WAGES, PRICES AND SOCIAL LEGISLATION IN THE SOVIET UNION

Lief Björk

WAGES, PRICES AND SOCIAL LEGISLATION IN THE SOVIET UNION

Translated from the Swedish by

M. A. MICHAEL

London

DENNIS DOBSON LTD

FIRST PUBLISHED IN GREAT BRITAIN IN 1953

Printed in Great Britain by the
BURLEIGH PRESS, LEWIN'S MEAD, BRISTOL
and published by DENNIS DOBSON LTD.
12 PARK PLACE, ST. JAMES'S, LONDON SW1

308/R

CONTENTS

5

CONTENTS

6

FOREWORD

In this book I have sought to give an account of certain parts of the social legislation of the Soviet Union, in particular of such regulations relative to the working conditions of the wage-earners as, according to Soviet terminology, fall within the sphere of 'labour justice' and which have been in, or have come into, force since the Second World War. The book also reports on the tasks and duties of the trade unions in so far as these are to be ascertained from the rules and regulations and similar documents, the regulations governing wages and social benefits, taxes, rents, prices of goods, etc. Certain statistics and tables are reproduced which have been taken from official publications.

The whole account—apart from certain personal observations—is based on information ascertainable either directly or indirectly from printed Soviet Russian sources, a list of which is contained in Appendix III. The main source of information has been the text of laws, directives, instructions, etc., and elucidations of them. In finding my way about this material I have been helped by the conversations I had and the observations I made in the spring of 1949 when I visited Moscow as the interpreter of the delegation of the Swedish TUC (Landsorganisationen), by information given me by people who have lived in the Soviet Union and by a study of non-Russian literature.

I should like to emphasize that a book of this kind cannot pretend to give a concrete picture of the conditions under which wage-earners live and work in the Soviet Union. The available statistical material is exceptionally meagre; and as far as concerns those figures and tables which I have quoted, it must be said that I have had no means of obtaining either detailed definitions or particulars of the methods of calculation used. The aim of the book is, first and foremost, to give as up-to-date as possible an account of the legal regulations in force in the sphere in question.

In certain accounts of the purport of laws, regulations, etc., I have retained the present tense in which the Russian text was written, but this does not necessarily mean that all such regulations were still in force when the book was completed. The most recent works in which the most important of these regulations are to be found are listed in Appendix III.

It has not been my aim to describe the practical application of Soviet legislation. In Soviet publications are to be found reports of infringements of current laws and accounts of individual cases that have been taken to court, but I have not found it possible to form any general opinion on the basis of such material.

It should be pointed out, too, that most of the regulations with which this book is concerned apply only to one part of the working population of the Soviet Union. There are separate regulations for the members of the collective farms and co-operative craft organizations, and for the many categories of persons interned in corrective labour camps.

In order to make it easier to understand this exposition and certain terms which are continually recurring, I have put together in Appendix II some explanatory notes about the administration and concerning legislation in other spheres than those dealt with in Chapters I–XII, as also certain statistical information.

The translation of the Russian terminology has proved far from easy, and unless the reader constantly bears in mind the fundamental differences between our social life and institutions and those of the Soviet Union, he may easily be led into misunderstandings by the inevitable use of some of our own terms.

CHAPTER I

INTRODUCTORY SURVEY

THE following chapters with their more detailed accounts of the development of social legislation in the Soviet Union after the Second World War require a background. This short survey of certain features in the growth of the Soviet social system and in its social legislation will, I hope, provide what is required.

In the period immediately subsequent to the revolution of November 1917 the economic and social policy of the Soviet State was that a number of the more important undertakings and industries were to be nationalized and private enterprise brought under public control. Shortly after the revolution, laws were promulgated restricting hours of work, making provision for unemployment and health insurance and holidays for wage-earners, etc.

War Communism

The inception of civil strife in the early summer of 1918 marked the beginning of that period in the economic policy of the Soviet State which is called 'war communism' and which led to a highly centralized war economy. Almost the whole of the country's industry was nationalized, the surplus production of agriculture was sequestered, and trade in commodities was largely replaced by distribution *in natura*. A large proportion of the civil population was mobilized for work after legislation had been passed, which made work the duty of all. The trade unions, membership of which during this period was compulsory, co-operated with the State officials in regulating conditions of work.

The New Economic Policy

In 1921 'war communism' was replaced by the 'new economic policy' (NEP), which restricted and decentralized the economic activities of the State and gave increased freedom of movement to individual and co-operative enterprise. According to the new labour legislation which was systematized in the ' labour code ' of 1922, a wage-earner's engagement should as a rule be based on a labour contract (*cf.* p. 36), and compulsory labour powers should only be used in exceptional circumstances, such as for dealing with natural catastrophes or where there was insufficient labour for tasks of special importance. The regulations making membership of a trade union compulsory were abolished and working conditions were to a large extent regulated by collective agreements, according to which the wages for different categories of workers and employees were graduated according to the professional skill required, the magnitude of the output, etc.; later statutory regulation of wage-conditions was introduced and these collective agreements became of less and less importance (*cf.* p 23). The centralized natural economy of 'war communism' was succeeded in the ' new economic policy ' by a market economy in which State, co-operative and private undertakings and private individuals figured as buyers and sellers.

The ' new economic policy ' meant that individual entrepreneurs in industry, trade, agriculture, etc. under certain conditions could employ paid labour. This form of private enterprise was progressively eliminated with the industrialization and collectivization of agriculture in the 1920's and 1930's, and economic life came to be entirely dominated by State enterprise, collective agriculture and co-operative organisations. A similar development has taken place in the new areas that have been incorporated into the Soviet Union since 1939.

Forms of undertakings in Soviet trade and industry

The major part of industry consists of State undertakings. The various State undertakings are under the control of central, regional or local authorities; they have a certain economic independence and freedom to conclude agreements, take on labour, etc. (*cf.* p 35).

The most important form of undertaking in agriculture is the collective farm, the *kolkhoz*. Alongside these there are State farms (*sovhoz*), some individual peasant-farmers (*jedinolichniki*) who are not attached to collective farms. The members of a collective farm can to a certain extent grow things for domestic consumption and for sale (*cf.* Chapter XII).

In the crafts there are both producer-co-operative associations (*artel*) and those who work on their own. Special permission is required before one can ply a craft as a private individual. Private craftsmen are not allowed to employ paid labour or apprentices in their craft (but they may employ members of their family). Numerous crafts are not allowed to be practised by private individuals, *inter alia* certain ones which involve the working up of purchased raw materials. It is, for example, permissible to make clothes and footgear for customers who provide the material, but not to make them of one's own; on the other hand it is permissible to manufacture furniture, ceramics, certain toys, etc. of one's own material for sale in the open market.

Any form of re-sale as a business is forbidden. On the other hand, craftsmen (in certain cases) and peasants (together with the members of their families) have the right to sell their products on the market. The forms of legal trade are discussed in greater detail in Chapter XII.

Apart from the forms of private occupation just mentioned, there are in the Soviet Union various ' free professions ', such as private practice as doctor, dentist, veterinary surgeon, nurse, masseur, typist, stenographer, teacher, etc., literary and artistic activities, etc. The legislation on taxation contains special regulations concerning this category of sources of income (*cf.* p. 100).

Population statistics

The population of Russia, or of that part within the frontiers of the Soviet Union as they were at the beginning of 1939, was on 1st January 1914 139·3 millions. At the census of December 1926 147·0 million persons were registered and at that of January 1939 170·5 million. The population in the new areas incorporated with the Soviet Union during 1939 and 1940 was *circa* 23 millions. Some further areas were added after the Second World War. In *Demographic Yearbook* 1949–50, issued by the United Nations, it is stated that in 1946 the population of the Soviet Union was officially calculated at *circa* 193 millions.

From 1926 to 1939 the population in the towns (including urban communities) increased from 26·3 to 55·9 millions, that is from 17·9 per cent of the total population to 32·8 per cent.

According to the 1939 census the population of the Soviet Union, other than in certain territories in the more northerly parts of the country, was thus divided among the various social groups (members of families included):

Workers	54,566,300
Employees	29,738,500
Collective agriculturalists	75,616,400
Craftsmen organized co-operatively ..	3,888,400
„ not „ „ ..	1,396,200
Private peasant farmers	3,018,000
Not working	60,000
Social position not given	1,235,300

Total .. 169,519,100

Published official statistics give the following particulars of the numbers of workers and employees, in millions :

1928 .. 11·6	1932 .. 22·9	1936 .. 25·8
1929 .. 12·2	1933 .. 22·3	1937 .. 27·0
1930 .. 14·5	1934 .. 23·7	1938 .. 27·8
1931 .. 19·4	1935 .. 24·8	1940 .. 31·5

The *Great Soviet Encyclopædia* gives the following figures for the numbers of workers and employees in various branches of industry in 1932 and 1937 (in thousands):

	1932	1937
Totals	22,942·8	26,989·5
Of which: industry	7,999·7	10,111·7
building	2,835·1	2,023·2
transport	2,040·1	2,773·8
agriculture	2,857·5	2,482·6
education	1,351·1	2,303·0
public health	647·2	1,117·6
trade	1,410·8	993·9
state and social institutions	1,833·5	1,743·3

14

According to the same source the numbers of female workers and employees increased during the period 1929–1937 from 3,304,000 to 9,357,000. In 1937 3,298,000 women were working in heavy industries, 1,252,000 in education and 725,000 in public health.

According to the central statistical office of the Soviet Union, the numbers of workers and employees increased in 1946 by 3 millions and annually thereafter by from 1 to 2 millions. At the end of 1950 the number of workers and employees reached 39·2 millions.

Development of labour legislation since the 1920's

The labour laws promulgated in connection with the change-over to the ' new economic policy ' at the beginning of the 1920's have been altered considerably since then. In the following chapters some account is given of various regulations from the *Labour Code* of 1922 and later legislation concerned with various special spheres. Here I shall give a brief account of certain aspects of the development of labour legislation with which it is useful to be familiar if one is to understand the background of the laws in force after the Second World War.

In 1927 the working-day was shortened for large groups of wage-earners (*cf*. Chapter IV).

The swift expansion of industry and of other State enterprises which began with the first Five-year Plan (1928–1932), was accompanied by a strong tendency to excessive fluctuations on the labour market and a number of measures were introduced in order to restrict the mobility of manpower and to make labour discipline more strict.

An edict of the People's Commissar for Labour dated 9th October 1930 directed that the payment of unemployment benefit by the social insurance was to cease and that unemployed persons who refused to accept work assigned to them should be removed from the register of the labour exchanges.

In an ordinance issued on 20th October 1930 the Central Committee of the Communist Party explained that unemployment had been ' liquidated ' completely as a result of the rapid industrialization and the development of *kolkhozes* and *sovhozes*, and that the shortage of labour in industry and other branches of commerce had caused a ' bottle-neck ' which was retarding the tempo of socialist construction. Because of this, the Central Committee recommended a number of measures for planning the supply of labour to industry and combating excessive mobility in the labour market (*tekuchest*). In connection with this the public labour exchanges were reorganized as ' cadre boards ' and given the task of organizing the training of qualified labour and the recruitment of labour for industry and transport. It was laid down that ' malicious disorganizers of production ' who arbitrarily and without sufficient reason left their employment in socialized undertakings and sought work from the cadre boards should for the next six months be assigned work within industry and transport. Special regulations were issued granting benefits to workers, technicians and engineers who distinguished themselves by giving their services in 'shock brigades' or in 'socialist competition' or who had worked for a longer period of time in one undertaking.

In 1931 edicts were promulgated for organized recruitment of labour for industry by means of contracts for seasonal employment of collective farm workers.

In 1932 an edict was issued making absenteeism an offence; according to this wage-earners who remained absent from work without sufficient reason for one day were to be dismissed and to lose the right to enjoy the dwelling granted along with their engagement.

An edict of June 1933 merged the former People's Commissariat for Labour with the Central Council of the Trade Unions (*cf.* p. 95).

On 28th December 1938 the Council of People's Commissars, the Central Committee of the Communist Party and the Central Council of the Trade Unions issued an edict concerning ' measures to be taken for the maintenance of labour discipline, the improvement of practices in State social insurance and for combating abuses in this sphere '.

According to this workers and employees who were away from work for less than a day without sufficient reason were to be reprimanded by the management of the undertaking or institution or warned that they might be dismissed, be transferred to other lower paid work for a maximum of three months or be placed in a lower category. Negligence, if repeated thrice within one month or four times in two consecutive months, was to bring dismissal.

It was further enacted that workers or employees who wished to end their employment should give one month's notice.

Workers and employees who had been assigned dwellings along with their employment were to be given notice to quit if they terminated their employment at their own request or if they were dismissed for an offence against discipline or for a crime.

The period of uninterrupted employment in one undertaking necessary to entitle one to a holiday was increased from five and a half months to eleven months.

Workers and employees with more than two years' uninterrupted employment had priority in obtaining places in rest homes.

Separate rules were laid down for persons in the employment of private employers, for example domestic servants and the staffs of concessionary undertakings.

Lastly, the edict of 28th December 1938 increased the existing differences in the scale of social insurance benefits for workers and employees based on the period of uninterrupted employment in the same undertaking and the total period of paid employment.

On 26th June 1940 the President of the Supreme Soviet issued a ukase concerning ' the change to a working-day of eight hours and a seven-day working-week and the prohibition of arbitrary leaving of undertakings and institutions by workers and employees '. By this the normal working-day of the majority of workers and employees in State, co-operative and social* organizations and institutions was increased from seven to eight hours (cf. Chapter IV). Enterprises and institutions with a six-day week changed to a seven-day week, i.e. every seventh day (as a rule Sunday) became a day of rest. Further, workers and employees in State, co-operative and social enterprises and institutions were forbidden arbitrarily to leave their work or to move to another place of work. To leave or change one's place of work required the

* The expression ' social organizations ' (otechestvennoi organizatsii) is meant in the following to include professional, political and cultural associations, etc.

permission of the director of the concern or of the head of the institution; in certain circumstances these were bound to grant this permission (*cf*. p. 40). Workers and employees who left an undertaking without permission were to be punished with a minimum of 2 months', or a maximum of 4 months', imprisonment. Those absent from work without sufficient reason were to be punished with a maximum of six months' 'corrective labour' in their place of work, their wage being reduced meanwhile by a maximum of 25 per cent (*cf*. p. 88). In this connection the previous regulations for the compulsory dismissal of 'truants' (*cf*. p. 89) were cancelled.

The ukase of the President of the Supreme Soviet of 2nd October 1940 concerning state reserves of manpower initiated a reorganization of the training and recruitment of qualified labour for industry (*cf*. p. 45).

A ukase of 19th October 1940 gave the People's Commissars powers to order certain categories of technicians, office workers and more qualified workers to transfer from one undertaking to another, no matter where situated. Wide use was made of this ukase during the war for the evacuation and transfer of industrial undertakings (*cf*. p. 43).

After the entry of the Soviet Union into the war in 1941 a number of regulations were issued, the purpose of which was to increase labour output and tighten up labour discipline. On 26th June 1941 orders were issued for obligatory overtime (as decided by the Government) of 1–3 hours a day. Holidays were abolished during the war and monetary compensation given instead; however, in 1944 holidays were reintroduced for persons under 16. Special regulations increased the strictness of the disciplinary codes in war industries, the railways, etc. During the war, regulations were issued allowing for the 'mobilization for labour' of the civil population and widening the application of labour-liability, as too were a number of orders concerning the finding of employment for disabled soldiers and workers.

After the capitulation of Germany the pre-war legislation regarding holidays was restored in its entirety, and the regulations concerning obligatory overtime and labour mobilization were annulled.

In March 1946 the Supreme Council passed a 'law for a five-year plan for the reconstruction and development of the economic life of the Soviet Union 1946–1950 '. Some particulars of what the five-year plan contained and of the results so far published are given in the following chapters and in Appendix II.

CHAPTER II

THE STRUCTURE AND FUNCTIONS OF TRADE UNION ORGANIZATIONS

THE great majority of wage-earners in the Soviet Union is attached to trade union organizations. Before the Second World War the trade union organizations comprised some 25 of the 30 millions of workers and officials. In April 1949 the number of members was given as exceeding 28.5 million.

On pp. 155–170 are given the rules for trade unions in the Soviet Union, which were accepted at the tenth All-Union Trade Congress of April 1949. Certain aspects of the activities of the trade union organizations are discussed in the following chapters. Here an account will be given of a number of the rules concerning the structure of trade union organizations and their tasks, and also some particulars of their activities, especially in those spheres not dealt with at any length later in the book.

Organization

The trade union organizations embrace all categories of wage-earners—employees, even those in leading positions, and workers—and also students at the higher educational establishments, at trade middle schools and at schools for occupational training. They are associated in unions for various branches of the economy (in the spring of 1949 there were 67 such unions) and these in their turn are affiliated to the All-Union Central Council of Trade Unions.

The normal primary organization comprises the workers and employees at a place of work. Where there are at least twenty-five members, a committee must be elected to conduct daily business, and this is called ' factory committee ', ' workshop committee ' or (in the case of offices, public institutions, etc.) ' house committee '; smaller organizations elect a ' union organizer '. In the larger organizations there can even be separate 'departmental committees ' or 'union bureaux', which conduct union work within the various departments of an undertaking or institution, as well as ' union group organizers ' for smaller groups like gangs or shifts, etc.

According to the rules, the primary organizations have to appoint, either by direct or by indirect election, executive organs to direct union activities within different territorial areas. Thus within the various unions there are committees for particular towns, departments, districts, provinces and republics (*cf.* p. 161) and also a central committee for the whole union. Besides this, there are formed within the districts, provinces and republics union councils to deal with questions that affect several unions at the same time. The highest executive organ of the collective trade union movement is the All-Union Central Council of Trade Unions, to which from now on we shall refer as the 'All-Union Council.'

Membership

Entrance into a trade union organization takes place after personal application and acceptance at a meeting of members. Members pay as an entrance fee and as their monthly contribution one per cent of their wages (sometimes to the nearest, and higher, round figure). Membership of a trade union brings with it certain material advantages. Thus, union wage-earners are entitled to larger social insurance benefits in the event of sickness, pregnancy and childbirth, etc., than those not members of a union, and they enjoy priority in obtaining admission to rest homes and ' sanatoria ', crèches, etc. (*cf.* Chapter X). They have the right to become members of the union's ' fund for mutual aid ', which grants loans and direct assistance, and can besides obtain support from the organization's own funds. They can obtain legal assistance through their union and they have the right to make use of its cultural and athletic institutions.

Tasks of the trade organization

As has already been mentioned, the People's Commissariat for Labour was merged with the Unions' Central Council in 1933, and as a result the trade unions took over the management of the State's social insurance and assumed control of workers' safety and protection. Social insurance is now administered by the trade unions in co-operation with the welfare authorities (see Chapter X); it is financed with subscriptions from the enterprises and is separate from the activities financed with the membership dues and other income of the trade union organizations (*cf.* p. 169).

The All-Union Council and the various unions themselves co-operate in the framing of legislation touching economic, social and cultural questions. According to the regulations, the All-Union Council has to work out and submit to the government draft legislation on, *inter alia*, wages, workers' protection and safety and social insurance. The All-Union Council promulgates, with the approval of the Government, the edicts, instructions and directives within the scope of labour legislation.

Otherwise, the tasks of the trade unions set out in the rules consist mainly of the following: to co-operate in the framing of working conditions and to endeavour to increase productivity and production; to see that laws and regulations concerning conditions of work are put into effect; to further and supervise various kinds of welfare measures for wage-earners; to organize educational work, sport and assistance for their members. It is stated in the rules that the trade union organizations ' perform all their work under the guidance of the Communist Party—the organizing and guiding force in the soviet community '.

The activities of the trade unions are largely based on the unpaid services of their members.

The chairman of the All-Union Council, V. Kuznetsov, said during the survey he gave at the All-Union Trades Union Congress in April 1949:

'Our active cadres grow day by day, acquire experience of social-political and organizational work and raise the level of their political knowledge. In the active cadres we have about 1 million group organizers, over 1,200,000 insurance delegates and social inspectors for workers' protection, over 1 million members in wage commissions and over 2 million voluntary social workers occupying themselves with welfare matters. In all, over 9 million trade union members take part in commissions, councils, etc.'

Collective agreements before the Second World War

In the 1920's and early 1930's wages and working conditions for workers and employees were largely settled by *collective agreement* between trade union and undertaking or authority. With the change over to a more strongly centralized planning of economic life the collective agreement became less important, since wages and working conditions were more and more being fixed by State directive. According to *The Labour Laws of the Soviet Union* 'wage-regulation by agreement played a dominant part during the first phase of the socialist state's development, especially after the transition to peaceful work for the reconstruction of economic life '; this, it says, reflects a certain degree of decentralization in economic life. ' In the second phase of the development of the socialist state, when our country's entire economic life was settled and directed according to a homogeneous plan, the dominant method was that of State standardization of wages, and this was used both for employees and workers. For employees the amount of the wage was based on fixed lists of appointments and fixed basic wages, which were laid down by the government or in accordance with government directive. Wages for workers were settled on the basis of tariffs which were similarly fixed by the government or in accordance with government directive '.

A more detailed account of the principles by which the State regulated wages is given in Chapter V.

From 1935–1946 no collective agreements were renewed; the wages of most wage-earners were revised during this time in accordance with State directives. In 1940 the Chairman of the All-Union Council, N. M. Shvernik, said: 'As the plan is the decisive factor in the development of our economic life, questions of wages cannot be solved outside of the plan or without reference to it. The collective agreement has thus become obsolete as a method of wage adjustment.'

Since 1947 local collective agreements have been made between State enterprises and trade unions, but these have an essentially different character than had the agreements made between the wars (*cf.* p. 12), since even after 1946 wages and general conditions of work have been settled by State directive. Thus, from now on when the phrase collective agreement is used it will be such local agreements that are meant.

Wage rates at places of work

A certain scope for local initiative is left in the application of the State directives on wage rates. Thus a concern can adopt to varying extent the different systems of piece work and bonus rewards, and the norms of output on which these are calculated are usually fixed at the place of work (*cf.* Chapter V).

One of the duties of the local trade union organizations is to check that the wage regulations in force are in fact being put into effect. Disputes concerning the pay of individual workers can be referred to 'conflict commissions' (see Chapter VIII). Local collective agreements can include clauses for the introduction of piece- and bonus wage systems for certain groups of workers (*cf.* pp. 31–2).

The Trade Wage Commissions

One of the main themes in Soviet Russian publications dealing with the activities of the trade organizations is that of the intimate connection between wage rate and endeavour to increase productivity. This can be best illustrated perhaps by quoting the main points in the instructions for union wage commissions issued in 1940 by the All-Union Council.

According to these instructions wage commissions were to be set up under the direction of the local factory-, workshop-, house- or departmental committees, and were, *inter alia*, to:

co-operate in the organization of 'socialist competition' among workers, engineers, technicians and employees;

inform the other workers of the experience of the Stakhanovites by organizing ' Stakhanov schools', giving lectures and other instruction in effective working methods, etc.;

help the administration of the concern to organize technical instruction;

investigate what the wage system in force had done towards

increasing productivity and improving the quality of production, check complaints from workers and employees concerning mistakes in their wage rates and put forward proposals for adjusting the wage system;

help the management of the concern to carry out measures which would adjust norms of work, supervise the revision of output norms, see that the management promptly puts into effect measures concerning organization and the technical side and suggestions from the workers, organize instruction—*inter alia* by means of the 'sponsorship' of Stakhanovites—for those workers who were not fulfilling their output norms, see that the management removes the hindrances that were preventing the workers and employees from fulfilling and exceeding their output norms;

try to put a stop to interruptions of work and production of defective goods ;

check the wage level for different occupational groups and take measures to correct faults in the relationship between the remuneration of the different groups ;

check that the workers are placed in the correct tariff classes and that workers and employees are employed in accordance with their qualifications;

co-operate in compiling tariff-qualification handbooks;

check that the government's edicts about wages are being put into effect and see that wages are calculated correctly;

work for the maintenance of labour discipline;

organize conferences on production;

support the workers, technicians and officials over inventions and proposals for rationalization.

Socialist Competition

The basis of *socialist competition* is the undertaking by individuals and groups to better their performance in various ways, *e.g.* to exceed the production planned, to improve the quality of the goods, to bring down costs, to lessen the amount of labour and material used, etc. The winners are rewarded with marks of distinction of various kinds and with material benefits (*cf.* Chapter V).

In the account of union activities he gave at the congress in April 1949, Kuznetsov said that socialist competition embraced over 90 per cent of all workers and employees; and he further said:

'Workers, engineers, technicians, employees assume individual obligations and compete with each other; there is competition between different teams and production departments and between the enterprises within a branch. Workers in the coal mines of the Donbas compete with the miners in Kuzbas, the oil workers in Baku with the oil workers in the east, the railwaymen on one line with those on another line. There is now competition for the place of the best ironworks-, steelworks- or rolling mills-section within metallurgical production.

'More and more are taking part in the competition between concerns in the various branches of industry that are situated within the same province, district or republic; all-union socialist competition between teams of workers in the same trade is growing increasingly extensive.'

In Soviet Russian publications the so-called Stakhanov movement is often called the highest form of socialist competition, and the term Stakhanovite includes, *inter alia*, workers who have taken initiative over more effective working methods, for example a more practical allocation of duties within a shift or gang. It was by such an act of initiative that the coal miner Alexei Stakhanov in 1935 increased the quantity of coal dug by his gang several-fold.

In conjunction with this socialist competition the trade unions carry out propaganda for technical education, rationalizing and the better organization of work.

'Factory committees, section committees and group organizations help the competitors to work out their undertakings, check the results of the socialist competition and publicize the experiences of those who have led in production. To do this they organize Stakhanov schools, arrange lectures and talks with the leaders in socialist competition, make propaganda for the results obtained by the Stakhanovites in factory newssheets, posters and also public books by Stakhanovites.' (Kuznetsov.)

Production Conferences

Another aspect of the work done to further technical progress and improve working methods is the *production conference*, which is organized by the local union organizations and at which directors of concerns and members of their staffs discuss the possibilities for technical improvements. In 1948 over two million such conferences were held in industry, transport, building and agriculture, and at them more than four million proposals for improved methods of production were accepted.

'Those attending the conferences put forward concrete, positive proposals which aim at removing faults in production, obviating stoppages in work, improving the quality of products and lowering the costs of production. The production conferences are of effective help in spreading knowledge of the experiences of the pioneers in production. They promote the application on a large scale of "fluid methods of manufacture", of automatic production, rapid smelting, rapid methods for metal working and other progressive measures '. (Kuznetsov.)

Social and cultural activity

The trade union organizations have to supervise the measures taken by concerns to procure dwellings for their employees and the management of the shops, eating-places, etc., which serve the workers and employees, and to do this have commissions, representatives, etc. They have to co-operate in the organization of the state-financed building of homes-to-own and also the cultivation of vegetables and keeping of animals, whether individual or collective.

The trade unions carry on a many-sided cultural activity which is financed in part by means of contributions from concerns and the State. At the beginning of 1949 the trade unions had at their disposal more than 8,000 clubs, houses and palaces of culture, more than 8,000 libraries, about 70,000 'red corners' at places of work and more than 5,000 cinemas. They arranged lectures on political, general and technical subjects, concerts, literary readings, dances, etc., and the sale of tickets for the cinemas, theatres and concerts. They organized study-circles and amateur groups for theatricals, singing, music, etc. At the beginning of 1949 there were some one and a half million members of circles for 'artistic personal activities' and more than five million members of all the various 'club-circles'.

The trade unions superintend the work done at crèches, kindergartens and homes for orphaned children. They engage in pedagogic activities among children of school age by organizing pioneer camps (*cf*. p. 129), playgrounds, circles for art, technics, nature study, etc.

The various athletic associations work under the direction of the trade unions. In 1948 these associations comprised some six per cent of all trade union members. In 1949 the trade unions had at their disposal more than 4,000 stadia, halls and athletic grounds and similar establishments.

Funds for Mutual Aid

A fund for mutual aid can be formed in conjunction with a union primary organization if at least 25 members are prepared to join it. Where so many are not available such funds can be organized with the regional committee of the trade union concerned. The activities of these funds are financed by means of subscriptions, income from interest and possible contributions from union organizations. The members of the funds pay an entrance fee of half per cent of their month's wages, and a monthly subscription of the same amount. During sickness they are relieved of the necessity to pay their subscription; those who have paid fifty monthly subscriptions can be freed from further payments.

The funds grant long-term loans at a maximum interest of six per cent to members who have belonged for at least two months, and also short-term loans to the next pay day. Members in need can obtain direct support, which is financed from the fund's income from interest. In judging applications for loans and support, the points to be taken into consideration are the applicant's need, how long he has been a member of the fund and how many subscriptions he has paid and the degree of punctuality in paying subscriptions and repaying previous loans.

Collective Agreements after the Second World War

Since 1947 collective agreements have been made annually between concerns in industry, transport and building on the one hand and their local union organs (factory-, workshop- or house-committees). Since 1948, agreements have also been made for the post, telephone and telegraph services, state agriculture and machinery and tractor stations. As has already been mentioned, these agreements are essentially different in character to those concluded during the inter-war period (cf. p. 12).

According to *The Labour Code of the Soviet Union* the predominant feature in the present agreements is 'the parties'' mutual concrete undertakings concerning the implementation of various measures which promote the fulfilment and surpassing of the economic plans, assist in improving working conditions and caring for the living and cultural requirements of the workers and employees.' On the other hand, they contain but few stipulations concerned with the working conditions of particular wage-carners. ' Thus, for example, the management undertakes to transfer workers to more qualified work as their professional skill increases, to promote the workers to a higher tariff class after they have passed tests, etc.' According to the same source, the collective agreements also contain 'moral-political' undertakings, some—mainly on the management's side—purely juridical obligations, the neglect of which can mean incurring legal penalties. 'Material liability' (obligation to pay) cannot be imposed on the union organizations arising out of stipulations in the collective agreements (cf. p 179).

An edict of the presidium of the All-Union Council concerning collective agreements for the year 1949 laid it down that in preparing draft agreements for individual undertakings, the basis taken should be the state plan for the productive activities of the concern, its welfare arrangements, etc., and also the directives prepared by the ministry concerned and the central committee of the trade union in question. The agreement should include undertakings from the management and factory committee on the following:

(a) Measures for the continued development of socialist competition, for the introduction of new technical methods, and utilization of experience gained by Stakhanovites, making better use of the production apparatus, lowering production costs and increasing the formation of capital.

(b) The management's undertakings in respect of the introduction of 'progressive norms' for the utilization of machinery, mechanisms and electrical sets, power, fuel, material and raw materials, which (norms) are achieved by the most capable workers, engineers and technicians and exceed the arithmetical average norms for the concern. On the basis of these norms, time-tables for the introduction of separate book-keeping for production departments, labour departments and shifts, have to be worked out and incorporated in the collective agreements.

(c) Measures for improving the organization of production, for systematizing the norming of work and for increasing the importance of theoretical output norms.

(d) Measures to improve the material welfare arrangements and cultural services for workers and employees, especially the younger and kithless, and also for better care of children by means of extending the system of crèches and other preparatory institutions.

(e) Steps to obtain building material, transport, labour, etc., for the provision of dwellings and the repair of dwellings.

(f) Steps to provide roads, parks, piped water and drainage, etc., in workers' communities.

(g) Dates for the construction of new and the reparation of existing dining-rooms, shops, store-rooms for vegetables, steps to have them equipped, to reduce the cost of meals for personnel, measures for improving the choice and for closer control of the quality of the goods delivered to 'departments for the provision of workers' (*cf.* Chapter XII).

(h) Preventive measures to reduce sickness, measures for the protection of workers and for hygiene, measures to improve the medical attention given to sick workers and employees.

Conditions of remuneration which had not been approved by the government might not be inserted in collective agreements.

Example of stipulations in collective agreements

In the 1948 collective agreement for the Stalin motor-car factory in Moscow the management undertook, *inter alia*, to complete the erection and put into use an overhead crane in one of the stores, to manufacture and erect four electric furnaces, install two hammers in the blacksmiths' shop, equip a hospital with 50–60 beds, open an establishment for medicinal baths, arrange for suction ventilation in the foundry and complete 12,500 square metres of dwelling space.

In 1947 the All-Union Council and the ministry for the transport machine industry prepared a draft collective agreement for the locomotive workshops in Kolomna, which was said to be the model agreement for the ministry's concerns. The agreement was said to include the following stipulations regarding remuneration and fixing of labour norms (*cf.* Chapter V).

As soon as a worker or employee is taken on, the management was to give him an account book and explain to him the wage regulations. The agreement gave the basic wages for different categories of workers, for example those working on time-rates and piece-rates in ' cold ' and ' hot ' work in the main departments, rules for calculating increments in different trades, etc. There was a separate list of which trade groups were to be remunerated in accordance with the tariff wages for ' hot ' work; certain groups of time-rate workers were to be remunerated in accordance with the rates in force for piece-workers.

The individual workers and the different kinds of workers were to be placed in tariff classes in accordance with a qualifications tariff given in a handbook prepared by the ministry in consultation with the All-Union Committee. As the workers improved their skill, the management was to move them to more qualified work and promote them to a higher tariff class as soon as they had passed the test. A worker who for three months in succession had done higher qualified work and in so doing fulfilled the output norms was entitled to be promoted to a higher tariff class after passing the tests.

Piece-workers doing work which was remunerated according to a tariff class at least two classes lower than the tariff class of the worker in question were to be given a supplement corresponding to the difference between their tariff wage rate and the rate for the work they were doing, provided that they fulfilled the output norms. The management was to undertake to introduce piece-rates for all work for which it was possible to fix norms.

The management was further to revise out-of-date output norms which did not correspond to production-technical conditions and to inform the workshop committee of this. New output norms and piece-rates were to be brought to the attention of the workers at least three days before they were introduced. If the norms had been revised in conjunction with the implementation of a proposal submitted by a worker (this presumably refers to suggestions for improving the organization of work or technical improvements), the worker submitting the proposal was to be remunerated for six months according to the piece-rates previously in force. During the period when a new production was being started, the management could fix temporary output norms and piece-rates, but both norms and rates were to be revised after three months at the most.

In the case of work of special importance it was permissible to employ a progressive piece-rate system according to regulations laid down by the Government. The management, in consultation with the workshop committee, was to draw up a list of such work and the provisions concerning the method of calculating the progressive increments and also their duration.

Certain categories of time-rate workers, like fitters, greasers, mechanics, etc., could receive special bonuses.

The workers must be informed three days in advance when progressive piece-rates or bonuses were to be introduced, and a fortnight in advance when they were to cease to be in force.

Engineers, technicians and other employees were to receive their wage, and possibly bonuses, for fulfilling the plan in accordance with the regulations laid down by the Government.

The agreement contained stipulations concerning the times when wages were to be paid.

The factory committee was systematically to check that the method of remuneration being used was in accordance with the statutes in force, and also to check the computation of the wages.

Observance of Collective Agreements

In V. Kuznetsov's report on union activities from which we have already quoted, he said that at meetings devoted to discussion of collective agreements 700,000 suggestions had been put forward in 1947 and over a million in 1948; more than half of these suggestions were concerned with improving ' production and the organization of work and payment for work.' Kuznetsov further said:

' However, in a number of factories and workshops the obligations assumed in the collective agreements were not satisfactorily fulfilled, this was especially so in regard to mechanization of work expensive in manpower, in putting into effect measures of technical organization and in the building of dwellings and premises for cultural and welfare activities.

' It is the duty of the trade union to see that collective agreements are concluded at the right time and to organize a daily check on their being carried out exactly and in their entirety.'

In this connection it should be mentioned that the newspaper of the All-Union Council, *Trud* (Work), often publishes complaints of faulty observance of the stipulations of collective agreements, inadequate observance of the labour laws and weaknesses in the working of the union organizations. As an example of this ' self-criticism ', here are a few extracts from an article on the confederational congress for workers in the machine-tools and instrument industry (*Trud*, 15th February 1951).

' The reports on activities and the speeches of the delegates provided information that is evidence of great progress in the manufacture of machines. . . . But several of the ministry's concerns are systematically failing to achieve the plan. Great losses are constantly being made because of inferior production, and the spread of modern working methods is proving very slow. People ask: What has the Unions' Central Committee and its wage department done to help the collectives in backward concerns? For example, reports have repeatedly reached the Central Committee from the Kirov workshop in Vitebsk that the labour code was being violated and the management taking no notice of the experiences gained by the Stakhanovites. . . . The

33

C

workshops committee asked for help, but the officials of the Central Committee did not even consider it necessary to answer their cry . . . The resolution of the preceding (fourth) congress concerning improved organization and mass labour has not been carried out either. Ten per cent of those working in concerns in the machine tools industry have still not become union members, and several union organizations have not completed the plan for the collection of members' subscriptions . . . The delegates to the congress devoted much attention to collective agreements. The chairman of the workshop committee of the Kirov workshop in Odessa, Comrade Semina, criticised the ministry for the machine-tool industry for causing by its own actions that several points in their mutual undertakings had not been fulfilled during the last few years. The chairman of the workshop committee of the Kirov works in Tbilisi, Comrade Gogelidze, said that for the last three years the management had not fulfilled its undertaking to build a new boilerhouse. A dwelling house for workers begun several years previously had not yet been completed. The workshop committee had turned to the Central Committee and to the ministry for help, but without result . . . The congress made it obvious that many workshop committees and managements of concerns only remembered the collective agreements when they were the subject of mass control. This state of affairs did not seem in any way to disturb the Central Committee of the Ministry. The question of the result of mass control of the observance of collective agreements for the year 1950 had not once been discussed either at the council meetings of the Central Committee or at the staff meetings of the ministry.' The article mentions that the congress elected a new Central Committee and Commission of Review with the object of improving union work.

In Appendix II mention is made of certain juridical points of view on the postwar collective agreements put forward in two articles by V. M. Dogadov.

CHAPTER III

Engagement and Dismissal of Workers

THE labour code of 1922 contained separate regulations on working conditions for (1) wage-earners (workers and employees), and (2) persons set to work in accordance with the regulations on compulsory labour. Chapters III–X deal in greater detail with the legislation affecting workers and employees. Of that concerning compulsory labour the following may be said here.

Duty to work

The authorities have the power to impose compulsory labour on certain categories of citizen for the purpose of combating natural catastrophes or in the event of a shortage of manpower for tasks of special social importance. Exempt from this obligation to work are, in time of peace, those under 18 years of age, men over 45 and women over 40, persons who have temporarily lost the ability to work owing to sickness or accident, the disabled, pregnant women eight weeks before and eight weeks after childbirth, nursing mothers and women with children under the age of 8 (in so far as no other member of the family can assume care of the child). During the Second World War compulsory work was imposed on certain categories previously exempt. Remuneration for the work carried out under these regulations is fixed by special arrangement.

The duty to work mentioned here (*trudovaya povinnost*) should not be confused with either ' corrective labour ' (*ispravitelno-trudovye raboti*; (*cf.* p. 176) or the ' labour mobilization ' (*trudovaya mobilizatsia*) of the civilian population which was carried out during the Second World War (*cf.* p. 18).

The right to engage paid labour is in Soviet law mainly reserved for ' juridical persons ' (*cf.* p. 170), that is to say state and co-operative institutions, 'social organizations' (*e.g.* trade, political, cultural, etc.) Private persons have the right to engage

35

paid labour for their personal service (*e.g.* domestic servants, secretaries or chauffeurs).

A person can become engaged as worker or clerk either through concluding a *labour agreement* with a person, concern, institution or such-like, or by administrative order, as when pupils from trade schools and higher educational institutions are directed to a specific place of work (*cf.* pp. 44–45).

The right of legal persons to engage workers and clerks is further controlled by directives from the authorities and organizations. Thus State concerns and institutions have the right to engage staff in accordance with fixed lists and planned figures for manpower.

In collective agriculture and artisan-co-operatives (*artels*) the work is largely performed by the members; the return for the members' work varies according to the results of the collective farm's, or *artel's* economic activity, and their working conditions are not regulated by the legislation dealing with the working conditions of wage-earners which this book discusses. These organizations are in certain events and to a limited extent able to engage paid labour.

Thus, collective farms have the right to engage those with special qualifications, *e.g.* agronomists, engineers and technicians. Temporary labour may be engaged for urgent work that cannot be completed by the members themselves by the appointed time, and also for building.

The artisans' *artels* have the right to engage paid labour for auxiliary work that does not constitute the chief purpose of the *artel's* activities and for work requiring special training. According to the normal regulations for *artels* the number of wage-earners should not exceed ten per cent of the number of members. In exceptional cases and with the permission of the State supervisory authority, paid labour may even be engaged for an *artel's* main production.

The Labour Contract

A labour contract (*trudovoi dogovor*) can be either a verbal or written agreement by which the one party (employee) receives employment with the other party (the employer) in the character of either worker or employee to perform work of a certain kind against payment. A distinction is made between labour contracts and such agreements concerning the performance of work that does not presuppose that the person performing it is engaged as worker or employee (for example, literary or artistic commissions). There is no labour contract when a person becomes a member of a collective farm (or of an artisans' *artel*), but there is if he receives employment with a collective farm without becoming a member (*cf.* p. 53).

For a labour contract to be binding, the parties must be agreed on certain ' necessary conditions '; over and above these, the contract may contain ' additional conditions '. According to the *Labour Laws of the Soviet Union* there are usually only two 'necessary conditions ' required, namely that the parties are agreed that the employee is to be engaged and that they have decided in what trade or what clerical position he shall work. The contract having been concluded, the employee's conditions of work are determined partly by the laws, ukases and other ' normative acts ' (*inter alia* wage tariffs) in force for the work in question, and partly by the conditions on which the two parties have agreed. The stipulations concerning wages, working-hours, etc. contained in a labour contract must not run counter to the law and other normative acts. In so far as wages and other conditions of employment are not regulated by normative acts, the labour contract is to contain stipulations governing them; thus, for example, the conditions of payment for domestic servants and the length of the working-day in the performance of incidental employment are settled in the labour contract. Besides the ' necessary conditions ' it is possible to include in the contract additional conditions specifying in greater detail the duties of the employee or his rights (*e.g.* the right to receive a dwelling in connection with his employment.)

Labour-books

Workers and employees are bound to present a *labour-book* to the management when taking up employment. The labour-book must contain particulars of the employee's name, age, training and trade (clerical grade or trade speciality), of his work and transfers from one concern to another, of the reasons for such transfers and of distinctions and rewards received. Persons taking paid employment for the first time must produce particulars of their last occupation from the administration of their dwelling-house or town soviet.

Acceptance for work

When a contract for employment has been concluded, the employer (the management) is under an obligation to provide the work agreed.

The final acceptance for work can however be preceded by a trial period of at the most six days for workers, two weeks for subordinate employees and one month for employees in responsible positions. The management must judge the result of the trial period and decide whether the person in question is to be finally engaged. A person considering himself to have been unjustly condemned can appeal against the decision to a court or to the conflict commission (*cf.* Chapter VIII).

Labour Contracts of Restricted Duration

As a rule a labour contract should be concluded without a time limit. Only in certain circumstances, which are laid down by law, may a labour contract be concluded for a specific period of time. This is the case with the organized recruiting by the ministry of labour reserves of labour from the countryside for industry, building and transport. Here contracts are generally made for at least a year. Such labour contracts have to contain special stipulations concerning benefits in connection with travel to another place (indemnification of travelling costs, subsistence allowance, advance of wages, guaranteed dwelling, etc.) and of benefits for those prolonging the labour contract (*e.g.* loan for building one's own home).

Labour contracts of restricted duration may be concluded for a season or for a chance job and also with workers and employees who work in certain remote districts.

When a contract for a restricted period has expired it can be replaced by a contract for an unrestricted period, if the employer and wage-earner agree that the wage-earner shall remain in his post.

Cancellation of Labour Contracts

A labour contract may be cancelled with the consent of the parties. Further, a labour contract may be cancelled at the request of the management, wage-earner or ' third party ' (*cf*. p. 41) in the circumstances laid down by law.

A labour contract can be cancelled at the request of the management in the following circumstances:

1. If the concern is being closed down or its staff reduced.

2. If work has been stopped for more than a month.

3. If the wage-earner is found unsuitable for the work by reason of insufficient skill, capacity, etc. Dismissal on such grounds must be confirmed by the conflict commission (*cf*. p. 94).

4. If the wage-earner without sufficient reason, intentionally or through negligence, repeatedly neglects to fulfil the obligations of his employment.

5. If the wage-earner commits a crime that is connected with his work and has been established by the sentence of a court, or if he has been under arrest for more than two months.

6. If the wage-earner has been absent from his work because of sickness longer than two months.

7. If in accordance with a decision of a court of justice or conflict commission a person previously occupying the position of the wage-earner is to be reinstated in that position.

8. If the wage-earner refuses to permit himself to be transferred to another place in those cases when such transference is not compulsory (*cf*. p. 43), provided that either the concern as a whole is being transferred to another place or the wage-earner's previous post has been abolished.

According to the ukase of 26th June 1940 workers and employees in state, co-operative and social concerns, institutions and organizations may not leave their employment without the permission of the management. According to the ukase and later regulations, the management is obliged to give such permission in the following cases:

1. Where the wage-earner in the opinion of an expert medical commission is unable to continue his previous work and the management cannot provide him with other suitable work in the same concern or institution. (By 'suitable' work should be understood here, according to the *Labour Laws of the Soviet Union*, such work as is suitable not only from the point of view of the state of his health, but also in regard to his occupational qualifications.)

2. Where the wage-earner receives the old-age pension (*cf.* Chapter X).

3. Where the wage-earner has won a place in a university college or trade middle school. In such cases the management is bound to permit him to leave ten days before teaching begins.

4. Where the wage-earner has won a place in the ' post-graduate school ' (*cf.* p. 44). In such case the management is bound to permit his departure at the latest one month after receiving information of his entrance into the post-graduate school.

5. Where a female wage-earner is married to a member of the armed forces and her husband is transferred to another district.

6. When a female wage-earner's husband is transferred to another district in accordance with the ukase of 19th October 1940 (*cf.* p. 43).

7. When the wage-earner's spouse, parents, son or daughter go to one of certain remote districts to work there and the wage-earner also wishes to go there.

8. When a disabled member of the armed forces of the Second World War wishes to go to the place where the members of his family are living, or the family of such a disabled person (spouse, child, parents) wishes to go to the place where the disabled person is living.

9. When a pregnant woman or a mother with a child under one year old wishes to transfer to another job in the place where she is residing.

10. On the expiry of a labour contract of limited duration.

11. When a concern which made a contract with the wage-earner in connection with ' organized recruiting ' (*cf.* p. 16), does not fulfil the stipulations of the contract.

In all cases where the management of a concern is legally required to grant a wage-earner's request to terminate his employment, in the event of its refusing to do so the wage-earner can appeal to the courts.

In other cases, where a wage-earner wishes to terminate his employment, the management of the concern or institution has to judge whether departure shall be permitted or not. If the management refuses to grant permission, the wage-earner can appeal against the management's decision to the superior organization or authority. Thus a wage-earner who has been refused permission to leave a state industrial concern can appeal against the decision to the management of the trust concerned; if the trust refuses to permit him to leave, he can have recourse to the supervisory board for the industry in question and finally to the ministry (*cf*. p. 96).

Finally, there are certain circumstances in which a labour contract can be cancelled at the instance of a 'third party', these are (1) at the request of trade union organizations (but not local ones), (2) if decided by certain authorities, such as the ministry for state supervision or the state inspectorate of commerce, (3) in accordance with a decision of the courts (see p. 39), (4) by calling up or acceptance as a volunteer into the armed forces.

Certain functionaries in the local trade union organizations may only be dismissed with the consent of the superior organ for the trade union in question.

The dismissal of pregnant women or lone women with children under one year of age is only allowed in exceptional cases and with the consent of the labour inspector or of the trade union at the place of work.

When a wage-earner terminates his employment, the management is bound to hand him his labour book with a note of the reason for his employment ceasing.

Departure Benefit

In certain cases a wage-earner who is dismissed has the right to so-called departure benefit (corresponding to 12 days' wages), for example if entering military service, when a former holder of the position is being reinstated, or when he has been dismissed for refusing to move to another district (*cf*. pp. 39 and 43).

Stipulation of function

When a person is given employment as a worker or employee, it is as a rule assumed that he is fulfilling a definite function in the concern. Each individual labour contract should include a stipulation as to the position or trade for which employment is being given (*cf.* p. 37). Correspondingly, the function to be fulfilled should be stated when pupils from trade schools or higher educational institutions are directed to a certain place of work. In either case, the function must be entered in the labour-book (*cf.* p. 37).

In certain cases an employee can be ordered to do work which is not covered by the function thus stipulated.

Transfer to another place of work or to another job

According to the Labour Code of 1922 a wage-earner could be transferred to another place of work only if he himself consented; certain exceptions to this rule have been inserted by subsequent edicts.

According to the model regulations for the internal organization of work in state, co-operative and social undertakings and institutions, laid down by the Soviet Government in 1941 (*cf.* p. 86), the management when allotting the work must so organize it that each worker and employee is employed as befits his trade speciality and qualifications. Each worker and employee is bound to perform all such work ordered by the management as belongs to his function (service or trade), and also such work as the labour rules and regulations in force entitle the management to transfer him to.

The management of State, co-operative and social undertakings and institutions has the right to transfer workers and employees to other work for a certain time in the event of stoppages in work or in other events, when the transfer is necessitated by ' necessities of production '. In stoppages of work the transfer may last as long as the stoppage continues, in other cases for a month at most. The same reasons permit of workers and employees being transferred even to another concern in the same place.

When wage-earners are transferred to other work because of a stoppage, it is not permitted to order qualified workers to undertake certain transport and scavenging work, etc. or qualified employees to perform unskilled work, except in cases when this is rendered imperative because of some natural catastrophe.

It is considered an offence against labour discipline if a wage-earner without sufficient reason refuses to allow himself to be transferred to other work when that is motivated by the reasons given here (stoppages, etc.).

Wage-earners whose ability to work has been reduced by sickness can be transferred to lighter work. In these cases assistance can be paid out of the funds of social insurance (cf. Chapter X).

Where there are medical reasons for doing so, pregnant women may request a transfer to lighter work, before the time when they are entitled to freedom from work, and in that event may retain the average wage they have been receiving for the last six months.

According to the model regulations for internal organization (cf. Chapter VIII) offences against labour discipline can be punished with transference to lower-paid work for a maximum of three months or to a lower grade for at the most one year.

A wage-earner who by reason of his capacity to work having diminished is not able satisfactorily to perform his previous work can be transferred to other permanent work in the same concern.

According to the ukase of 19th October 1940 the People's Commissars (now Ministers) in the Soviet Union have the right to transfer engineers, designers, technicians, foremen, draughtsmen, book-keepers, economists, accountancy-, finance- and planning-staff as well as skilled workers in the seventh and higher tariff classes from one concern belonging to the ministry to another, irrespective of where the latter is situated. Similar regulations have since been introduced for certain central authorities and ministries in the different republics of the union. Refusal to let oneself be transferred is punished similarly to ' arbitrary departure ' from work (cf. p. 88).

A wage-earner who consents to be transferred to a concern in another area has to be given compensation for the costs of the journey (his own and his family's), a daily allowance while travelling, wages while travelling and for a further six days, plus a single payment of the equivalent of one month's wages at the new place of work for himself and one quarter of that amount for each member of his family travelling with him. If the wage-earner is transferred compulsorily under the ukase of 19th October 1940 the single payment to the wage-earner himself is increased to four months' wages (at the previous place of work) if being transferred to certain remote areas from other parts of the Soviet Union, and three months' wages in all other cases; if the transfer is connected with a disciplinary punishment involving reduction to a lower grade, this sum is reduced by half.

Training and placing of qualified labour

In the labour market a special position is accorded to the 'young specialists' who pass out from the trade middle schools and the higher educational institutes, and those qualified workers trained at the craft schools who come under the Ministry for Labour Reserves.

In the Soviet Union attendance at school becomes compulsory at the age of seven. In 1949 regulations were issued making instruction at school universal and obligatory for a period of seven years; previously this had been limited in country districts to four years. There are three main types of general schools, primary schools (classes 1–4), incomplete middle schools (classes 1–7) and middle schools (classes 1–10, or as in Georgia, Esthonia and Latvia, etc. classes 1–11); the lower classes in the middle schools correspond to those of the primary school.

The trade middle schools train technicians, nurses, teachers for primary schools and other 'specialists with middle school qualifications'. Instruction at these schools is usually based on the seventh class of the general school and continues for three or four years.

The higher-educational institutions take pupils who have passed through ten classes in the general school or who have passed out from a trade middle school. At the so-called aspirant (post-graduate) schools students who have passed the examination of a higher educational institute are trained to become university teachers and scientifically trained personnel.

At the end of 1950 there were 37 million pupils in the general schools (primary schools, seven-year schools and middle schools) and at the technical and other trade middle schools. At the higher educational institutions there were studying in 1950 1,247,000 students (including those taking correspondence courses).

Those who have finished their education at trade middle-schools or high schools are bound to work for at least three years at the place of work to which the ministry or authority concerned directs them. Any person not reporting to the place of work to which he has been directed is punished for 'arbitrary departure' in accordance with the ukase of 26th June 1940 (*cf.* p. 88). During this three-year period those who have passed their examinations are not allowed to request permission to leave in order to study at another educational institution. In general they have the same conditions of work as the other wage-earners. Those who are directed after their examination to work in another area receive compensation for the costs of moving.

State Labour Reserves

In conjunction with the ukase of 2nd October 1940 concerning state labour reserves (p. 18) a system of occupational schools has been set up for the training of qualified workers in industry and transport. The system comprises both schools which train qualified workers for the metal, chemical, mining and oil industries, the railways, etc., and factory- and workshop-schools for the training of workers in the 'mass trades'. The period of training varies for the different types of school from six months to four years.

The pupils in these schools consist of young persons of from 14 to 18 years of age. Admission follows on application or by being called-up ('mobilization',) and this is done by the town soviet and the president of the agricultural collective. Training is free; the pupils receive free board, clothes, shoes, bedclothes and all instructional material, as well as lodging for those who come from a different place. On completing their training, the pupils are obliged to work in state concerns for four years, and they are directed to these by the Ministry of Labour Reserves. During this four-year period these workers have their military service deferred. They have to be given work on the same conditions as are in force for the other wage-earners (except for their

45

obligation to work for four years at the place to which they have been directed) and they may not be placed in a lower tariff class (see p. 31) than that given them on passing their examination. They may be directed only to places where suitable accommodation is to be had.

The *Soviet Union's Administrative Law* (published 1950) gives the following details of the regulations for recruiting pupils for the occupational schools: for every hundred male and female members of collective farms between the ages of 14 and 55 the president of an agricultural collective must each year by calling-up order (mobilization) select two persons between the ages of 14 and 17 for artisan and railway schools, and two persons between the ages of 16 and 18 for factory- and workshop-schools. The town soviets are similarly to select young persons for the artisan-, railway-, factory- and workshop-schools, the number being fixed annually by the Council of Ministers (*cf.* p. 172).

According to the Five-Year Plan, four and a half million young qualified workers were to be trained at the schools for 'labour reserves' during the years 1946–1950. According to the statistical report of the Central Administration some 2,900,000 young workers were trained during 1946–1949 and in 1950 494,000, and were placed in industry, building and transport.

Mobility in the Labour Market

By making use of the legislation that has just been sketched, the central authorities have been able to direct certain categories of workers and employees to different undertakings. At the same time the undertakings have been able to engage labour without the agency of the authorities. Vacant positions have been advertised in the Press, on hoardings, etc. Latterly there have often been complaints over the 'over-mobility' (*tekuchest*) of labour in the Press and other publications. As an example, here is an extract from an article by E. Mochova on labour reserves: 'The facts show that the chief causes of over-mobility among the young workers, which in many cases has not yet been overcome, are to be found in the fact that these young workers' services are not properly made use of and that sufficient attention is not paid to their material living conditions. Workers' over-mobility involves the state in huge losses, prevents a planned distribution of labour and acts as a brake on increased production. For these reasons the economic leaders, the party, komsomol and trade organizations must devote the maximum of care to the young workers. First and foremost must they be helped to learn how to master the output norms. . . .'

CHAPTER IV

HOURS OF WORK AND FREE TIME

Legislation on Hours of Work

ON 29th October 1917 the Soviet Government issued a decree making eight hours the normal working-day for all wage-earners. Shorter hours were decreed for minors and for certain occupations injurious to health.

The Central Executive Committee of the Soviet Union issued on 15th October 1927, in connection with the ten-year jubilee of the revolution, a manifesto according to which the normal working-day was gradually to be changed from eight to seven hours.

By 1939 the seven-hour day had been introduced for the great majority of workers. The eight-hour day was still in force for certain groups, such as builders, workers on State farms, certain seasonal workers, lumber-workers, etc. Certain categories of employees, workers in noxious occupations and those between the ages of 16 and 18 had a working-day of six hours, and, in certain exceptional cases even shorter. For those between the ages of 14 and 16 the working-day was limited to four hours. The number of working-days in the year differed from group to group. Thus, certain concerns adopted an 'unbroken five-day week' with every fifth day free, while others had a six- or seven-day week.

According to the ukase of 26 June 1940, which we have already mentioned (p. 17), the normal hours worked by the majority of workers and employees in State, co-operative and social undertakings and institutions are eight a day. In the case of certain work underground, among other jobs, the normal working-day was seven hours, in noxious occupations (specially listed) six hours or in certain cases five or four hours. An even shorter working-day was fixed for certain intellectual professions, *e.g.* six hours for college teachers and from five and a half to seven hours for certain medical personnel; these professional workers can—like other wage-earners—augment their income through subsidiary occupations. Since 1940 the traditional seven-day week has been generally adopted.

In concerns working on the three-shift system the night shift may be shortened to seven hours; this, however, does not apply to continual working (*e.g.* power stations).

The working period may be shortened through pauses, *e.g.* suckling pauses for mothers or warming-up pauses for those working in the open during the cold season.

The normal working-day may be extended beyond the eight hours for certain seasonal work, *inter alia* log-floating.

Certain categories of wage-earners, like responsible political and trade functionaries, certain administrative personnel, chauffeurs, coachmen, linesmen, etc. have ' a non-normed working-day ', that is to say the length of time worked is determined by the amount of work that has to be done.

Overtime

Overtime may legally be prescribed in the following cases:

(a) for work that is essential for the defence of the country or for the prevention of disasters (fire, epidemics, etc.);

(b) for socially necessary work in repairing or restoring water supplies, light, drains, transport, postal, telephonic and telegraphic communications;

(c) for finishing a job that has been begun but which by reason of some unforeseen or fortuitous interruption in production due to technical causes it has not been possible to finish in normal working-hours, in so far as not to finish it would entail damage to material or machinery;

(d) for the repair and restoration of machinery and installations, if their stoppage involves interrupting the work of a considerable number of workers.

Further, a management has the right to retain a shift-worker until the arrival of his relief; in such cases, however, the management is bound to take immediate action to obtain a substitute.

Wage-earners are bound to work what overtime they are ordered to do.

D

Overtime cannot be ordered for young persons under 16, nursing mothers, pregnant women (from and including the fifth month) or persons with tuberculosis in an active form. Persons disabled either in war or industry may not be made to work overtime.

The number of hours of overtime that a wage-earner may work is generally limited to 120 hours per annum and 4 hours in any period of 48 hours. In seasonal work and building, as well as in the lumber industry and forestry, overtime may be imposed in excess of these limits.

The reward for overtime shall as a rule take the form of increased wage (see p. 64).

Days Off

As has already been stated, the traditional seven-day week was re-introduced in 1940. Wage earners have one day in the week off, usually on the Sunday. Other general days-off (holidays) are 1st January (New Year's Day), 1st/2nd May, 7th/8th November (Anniversary of the Revolution) and 5th December (day of the Stalin Constitution). Sunday work is usually compensated with time-off, holiday work with double wages or time-off.

Holidays

Workers and employees who have worked for eleven months without interruption with the same concern or institution are entitled to a holiday (time-off with pay).

It is not all work that an employee performs in a concern which constitutes the uninterrupted period of work which gives the right to a holiday. If a worker is condemned to corrective labour at his place of work (cf. p. 18) the duration of the punishment is not included in the qualifying period, but once he has worked out his punishment, the worker may claim the benefit of the time he worked in the concern before being sentenced (that is to say that the period of punishment is leap-frogged in reckoning the period of uninterrupted work). It is not permitted while serving a sentence to take a holiday previously earned.

On the other hand, in the qualifying period entitling a person to a vacation is reckoned the time a wage-earner may have been:

(1) Absent from the concern yet entitled to retain his position and—wholely or in part—his wage (as while performing military service or having leave of absence for a public mission) ;

(2) absent by reason of sickness or such cause, but retaining his position and receiving assistance from the social insurance;

(3) absent by reason of unjust dismissal;

(4) studying at a factory- or workshop-school (*cf*. p. 45).

With these exceptions, a period of eleven months of unbroken service with the same concern is generally stipulated as a condition for being granted leave. A wage-earner who is transferred to another concern or who has changed his place of work at the suggestion of the party-, komsomol- or union-organization is none the less permitted to count his period of service in his previous place of work in reckoning his qualifying period.

Workers and employees engaged on jobs of short duration —seasonal workers and such-like—are in general not entitled to holidays. Those who have worked on one and the same building for less than eleven months (but more than one month) do however receive instead of holidays compensation of four per cent of their wages during the time they have worked.

Holiday pay is reckoned on the basis of the wage-earner's average income for the last twelve months or from and including the first calendar month after being given employment with that concern. In this are counted all earned income, including bonuses, additions for overtime, age-bonus, etc., etc. and even benefits received from social insurance by reason of temporary loss of ability to work. On the other hand, travelling expenses for service journeys, compensation for holidays not taken, benefits received *in natura*, and such-like, are not included.

Holidays are in general to be granted every year. If the absence of a wage-earner were to have unfavourable effects on the course of the work being done, the management can postpone the holiday to the following year or pay cash compensation, this however requires the consent of the wage-earner or the approval of the conflict commission.

One must distinguish between *ordinary holiday* and *bonus holidays*. The ordinary holiday is normally 12 working-days. Certain categories of workers and employees enjoy *extended ordinary holidays* of 24 working days or longer. Wage-earners under 16 years of age have a holiday of one month. Certain members of the staffs of research institutes, teaching institutions and cultural institutions have holidays of from 24–48 working days. Teachers at schools and higher educational establishments receive 48 days holiday, if they have served the entire school-year.

Bonus holidays are granted to persons in strenuous and noxious occupations; for example typists who are constantly working at a typewriter receive a bonus of 6 working days, welders working in an enclosed space 12 days; medical personnel in institutions for child psychiatry, for psychically retarded children, etc. 36 days.

Further, bonus holidays can be granted as compensation for those working in remote parts of the country, as a reward for long service with one and the same concern, as compensation for changed working time and as a benefit for wage-earners who are studying while working or who have won admission to higher institutions of learning, etc., etc.

CHAPTER V

THE WAGE SYSTEM

IT has already been explained in Chapter II that general wage-conditions for workers and employees in the Soviet Union are nowadays usually fixed by state directive. There are, however, certain exceptions. Thus, the wages of those employed by individuals (*e.g.* domestic servants, secretaries and chauffeurs) and by collective farms (*e.g.* herdsmen and herd-boys) are fixed by individual agreement. The central regulation of wages for those in state service allows, however, as has been mentioned (*cf.* p. 24) certain room for local initiative in the choice of wage-system to be adopted, regulation of piece-work rates, classification of individual wage-earners in the wage-system, etc.

Chapter II also gave certain information on the workings of the union wage commissions, while the rules for dealing with disputes concerning the remuneration of individual employers are discussed in Chapter VIII. The present chapter seeks to give an account of the development of state wage-regulation and examples of different regulations.

State Regulation of Wages

State wage-regulation has been shaped with the object of stimulating wage-earners to increase their output and improve their skill. This is given expression in the differentiation of wage-income for the various occupational groups and in bonuses and other extra wages intended to stimulate output. The purpose of the differentiation in the wages of the various branches of commerce and industry as between different regions has been to increase the supply of labour to spheres of special importance for the country's economic development.

The principles of wage policy mentioned here were developed under pressure of the process of industrialization in the 1930's. During the war the difference in real income between various groups of wage-earners was less pronounced than the difference in money-income, because of the violent upset to the price level. While the prices of rationed goods were being kept more or less at the pre-war level, prices on the open market increased several-fold. In September 1946, as a preliminary to the abolishing of rationing—which did take place in December 1947—the prices of rationed goods were raised and those of goods on the open market lowered. At the same time an edict was promulgated giving additional wages to workers and employees with a monthly income of up to 900 roubles in accordance with the following scale:

Monthly Income (roubles)	Additional Wage per Month (roubles)
Up to 300	110
301–500	100
501–700	90
701–900	80

The tariffs and wage regulations previously in force were adjusted to include this ' dear-times increment ' and in consequence the discrepancy between basic wages for the lower and higher qualified work was reduced all along the line. For example, in certain tariffs for workers in the engineering industry, according to which the basic wage for the highest tariff-class had previously been 3·2 or 3·6 times as high as the basic wage for the lowest tariff-class, the corresponding proportions after the reform were 2·1 and 2·65.

Workers' Wages

Wages for *workers* are usually fixed by means of a ' tariff-net ', *i.e.* a table of basic wages for the different categories. The authorities concerned with each branch of industry co-operate with the union organizations to work out a ' tariff-qualifications-handbook ' which gives the principles on which the workers are to be divided in *tariff-classes* in accordance with the nature of their jobs and the responsibility, knowledge and skill required of them. The number of tariff-classes within an industry depends on the character of the production; there are, for example, 12 for foundries, 7 in the building industry, and in the tea industry 4. The allocation of the individual worker to his tariff-class is a matter partly of the work being performed and partly of degree of experience and of ability tests that he has passed. In certain branches of industry, as in the coal industry, the place of the 'tariff-net' is taken by direct rules for basic wages for the different special jobs.

Within each tariff-class and for every occupation—among both workers and employees—wage-conditions are the same for women as for men.

The following extract from a tariff-qualifications handbook for factories manufacturing machinery for the coal industry will serve as an example:

'*Draughtsmen in the third tariff-class*—

must be familiar with drawing-instruments, the rules for their use and care and have elementary knowledge of plane-geometrical constructions (drawing of parallels and lines at right-angles and such-like);
must be able from drawings and sketches to engrave smaller and not complicated details on a flat surface using simple instruments; under supervision of a first engraver to engrave more complicated details with independent drawing of working parts in the plane and emendation adjustment to water-level, rule and set-square; to assist the first draughtsman.

Examples of work:

1. Boring-machine—drawing of head for bit-brace and socket for holder.

2. Bolt for drive PK-19—drawing for cotter-hole.

3. Spanners—drawing for the mouth according to pattern.

4. Drawing for grooving of a cog-wheel, sockets and boxes for threshing machine and combine.'

One or more tariff-wage rates are fixed for each tariff-class : these refer either to wages by the hour (or day) for payment by time or basic wages (normal wages) for piece-work; in the latter case the tariff-wage is the basic rate for piece-rates. Tariff-wages are usually somewhat higher for piece-workers than for those paid by the hour or day who come within the same tariff-class.

As an illustration of this we reproduce here from the draft collective agreement for the year 1947 the following wage-provisions for workers in the main department of the locomotive workshops in Kolomna.

The workers were to be divided into eight tariff-classes within each one of the following 4 groups: (a) time-rate workers on ' cold ' work; (b) time-rate workers on ' hot ' work (in the foundry, blacksmith's shops, etc.); (c) piece-rate workers on ' cold ' work; (d) piece-rate workers on ' hot ' work. The following basic wages were to apply to these groups (roubles per hour):

Tariff-class	1	2	3	4	5	6	7	8
group (a)	1.20	1.33	1.50	1.70	1.88	2.14	2.47	2.86
„ (b)	1.28	1.43	1.61	1.84	2.05	2.34	2.71	3.08
„ (c)	1.37	1.54	1.74	1.99	2.24	2.57	2.93	3.43
„ (d)	1.50	1.70	1.93	2.17	2.51	2.89	3.32	3.85

Piece-work and output norms

Piece-wages are adopted for most of the productive workers in industry, so that the wage-income is either directly proportional to the output or rises more than proportionally when the output exceeds a certain limit ('progressive piece-wage '). In either case the wage is calculated on the basis of 'output norms', 'time-norms', etc., fixed with regard to the varying technical and organizational circumstances of each place of work.

The output-norm is the number of products a worker should produce or the number of operations he should perform in a certain period of time under normal working-conditions (*i.e.* when the machines are in order, the material coming forward at the right time, etc.). For example, for bricklayers there may be fixed a norm of 1,000 bricks in eight hours.

The time-norm is the time a worker should take to produce a certain product or carry out a certain operation under normal working conditions. Thus time-norms are the inverted value of the corresponding output-norm. For example, a turner can be set to turn ball-bearings with a norm of 20 minutes each.

In Soviet publications a distinction is usually made between ' norms based on experience-statistics ', the basis for which is the experience of managements and particulars of previous average outputs, and ' technically-based norms ' (theoretical norms) worked out on the basis of studies of the technical process, and capacity of the equipment, exact time-studies of the time taken by the various operations, the experience of Stakhanovites, etc. The law for the Five-years Plan 1946–1950 emphasized the necessity for more extensive adoption of theoretical norms within industry.

The following are extracts from *The Labour Laws of the Soviet Union* concerning the principles and methods for determining and adjusting norms:

'Output-norms should be an expression of the level of technical development and of the organization of production; they ought to be averagely progressive; they must reflect and universalize the experience gained by those workers who have been promoted, the increase of skill and raising the cultural and technical level of the working class. It follows from this that the output-norms must be periodically revised and replaced by higher norms.

'For the present the regulations for the revision of output-norms are laid down in the edict of 14th January 1939 promulgated by the Council of the People's Commissars of the Soviet Union. General directions for the revision of output-norms for all supervisory boards within a certain ministry are drawn up jointly by the minister and the All-Union Council. On the basis of such directives the heads of the supervisory boards, jointly with the chairman of the central committee of the trade union concerned, draws up directions for the revision of output-norms in the various undertakings.

'In each undertaking the director fixes the output-norms after consultation with the departmental chiefs. The moment these have confirmed them the new norms come into force and are brought to the knowledge of the workers. New norms remain in force for a year. When the organization of production is changed or technical alterations made or rationalizing measures taken, which increase the productivity of labour, the output-norms ought to be raised correspondingly.'

As already mentioned (p. 25), the union wage commissions at the various places of work have to co-operate in the implementation of measures concerned with the norming of work.

In April 1946 the All-Union Council plenum passed a resolution concerning the duties of the union organizations in connection with the execution of the Five-year Plan for 1946–1950, in which it was stated, *inter alia*:

'It is the duty of the trade unions' central, provincial, factory-, workshop- and house-committees daily to occupy themselves with wage-questions, to make sure that the system of remuneration in force is being applied in the right way, to remove what may be preventing the workers from increasing the productivity of their labour and thus their own reward; to work for a more general application of the piece-wage system and progressive piece-wage system and also of theoretical output-norms instead of those based on experience and statistics, as well as for a revision of out-of-date tariff-qualification hand-books.'

Calculation of piece-wages

Piece-wages are calculated per product unit on the basis of the norms and the tariff-wages for the various workers. In certain cases (*e.g.* in the building industry) a lump sum is fixed for work of greater size.

With ordinary piece-work one and the same piece-wage applies irrespective of how much the worker produces per unit of time. With progressive piece-wages the piece-rate rises in accordance with a certain scale; this occurs either after exceeding the norm or when the worker has passed a lower 'starting-basis', *e.g.* 80 per cent of the norm. According to the draft collective agreement for the locomotive workshops in Kolomna, to which reference has already been made, the progressive system of piece-rates was to be adopted for work of special importance. In the case of 'cold' manual work the piece-wages for that part of the production which exceeded the fixed hourly norm (or possibly another 'starting-basis') were to be raised by respectively 25, 50 or 100 per cent if the norm (starting-basis) were exceeded by 1–10, 11–25 or more than 25 per cent. In the case of 'hot' work, the corresponding addition to the piece-rates was to be 50, 100 and 200 per cent.

In the case of team-or group-work an output norm was fixed

for the entire team, and payment calculated on the collective output and distributed according to the time the various members of the team had worked and their tariff-wage rates.

It is often possible for those working on time-rates to receive a bonus for good results in addition to the basic wage fixed by the tariffs. Thus, for example, greasers and repairers can receive an additional bonus if the number of stoppages is reduced. A charwoman can receive a proportional extra wage for exemplary work. Both workers and employees can receive prizes for suggesting measures resulting in saving or rationalization (*cf.* p. 25).

Promotion to a higher tariff class

The individual worker has a direct economic interest in obtaining promotion to a higher tariff-class. Such promotion may be made, for example, with the worker being transferred to more difficult work for which he has acquired the experience or by his passing tests after taking training-courses.

In her autobiography, Anna Kuznetsova, a young Stakhanovite in a motor-car-factory, tells how she was qualified as a driller in the third tariff-class after passing an examination on completing a ' technical minimi-course '. Later she took a course for ' multiple-machine workers '; rose to the fourth tariff-class and began to work two machines.

Apparently the systems of tariff classification differ considerably. V. Manevich maintained in an article in *Voprosy ekonomiki* (1948, No. 10). ' In most of the concerns in the ministry for the heavy machine industry no workers at all are placed in the first tariff-class. The relative number of workers in the second tariff-class is somewhere between 0·9 and 6·1 per cent. In many concerns charwomen are placed in the third and even the fourth tariff-class, and odd-job men are not placed lower than in the fourth class. Such a classification does a concern considerable damage; a manipulated abuse of the tariff-classes is one of the causes of the illegal overstepping of the wage-budget, and, besides that, it weakens the incentive for workers to improve their qualifications. Not unfrequently there is but the slightest supervision by management or union organization of the promotion of workers to higher tariff-classes. Yet the promotion of workers to higher tariff-classes after passing their tests is a tremendous incentive for the workers to increase their output and to learn to master various special jobs.'

Basic wages and real incomes

Whatever his tariff-class the worker's real income may be very different to the basic wage given in the tariff. It is well-known that Stakhanovites can often achieve monthly incomes that are several times their tariff-wage and can amount to several thousand roubles. Mention is made, for example, in *The Labour Laws of the Soviet Union* of a miner in Donbas, who for the three months January to March 1948 earned 6,302, 6,517 and 7,712 roubles respectively.

The majority of workers in industry are on piece-rates. According to *The Labour Laws of the Soviet Union* (1949 edition), the piece-rate system was adopted for 71 per cent of the workers in enterprises coming under the ministry for the machine-tool industry, for 83 per cent of those in the cotton industry, and for 92 per cent of those in the lumbering industry.

As the law is, a piece-rate worker who through his own fault does not achieve the output-norm fixed for him is to be paid proportionately to his output in accordance with the piece-rates in force. If he falls below the norm because of circumstances outside his control, he is to receive at least two-thirds of his tariff-wage; separate regulations deal with stoppages and with cases where the product is below standard (*cf.* pp. 63–4).

Wages for employees

The wages for employees are usually fixed in accordance with a nomenclature of posts laid down by the government, service-lists for each concern or institution and definite basic-wages for each post.

In certain cases the wage for a post may lie between given maximum and minimum limits, and then the management has the right to fix the wage for the individual employee within these limits having regard to his qualifications and the nature of his work.

The fixed basic-wages for employees are differentiated with regard to such circumstances as the compass of the work (*e.g.* the number of beds in a hospital, the turnover of a shop, the number of subordinate employees), qualification (extent of service training) and responsibility (official standing, importance of the work, etc.). In certain cases a difference in wage is made for various geographical areas. Certain central authorities may fix higher ' personal wages ' for highly qualified officers.

Bonus

There are various kinds of bonus that employees may receive in addition to their fixed basic-wage. Thus, for example, heads of concerns, technicians and foremen—as also workers—in state industries are given a bonus for ideas that result in a saving of fuel, heat and electrical energy.

Heads of concerns and technicians in industry may also receive a bonus if their undertaking or individual production-department fulfils or betters the planned volume or cost of production, the assortment of products, etc. Thus, for example, in certain factories the director is given an extra fifty per cent of his salary if the concern fulfils its production plan, and a further 5 per cent of his salary for every one per cent that the plan is exceeded. Thus, a director with a basic salary of 3,000 roubles a month can, if production is 15 per cent more than that planned, receive an additional 1,500 roubles for achieving the planned production and 2,250 roubles for exceeding it, giving him a total monthly income of 6,750 roubles. Correspondingly a foreman, for example, with a basic-wage of 900 roubles can receive a bonus of 270 roubles (30 per cent) if his department fulfils its plan, and a further 810 roubles (3 x 30 per cent) if the plan is exceeded by 30 per cent; his monthly wage thus becomes 1,980 roubles.

Director's Fund

It is necessary to distinguish between the bonuses that are part of the wage-system itself and paid out periodically, and the special payments made to individual employees at the discretion of the management for special performance. Such rewards are made out of the so-called *director's fund* which most state industrial concerns have and which are separately accounted for. The fund has an appropriation varying from 2 to 10 per cent of the profit or reduction in costs planned for each year plus 25 to 75 per cent of the profit or reduction in costs in excess of that planned, assuming that the concern has fulfilled the state plan in respect of quality and assortment of products as well as of costs and output.

The fund's resources are to be used for the expansion of production, the erection and maintenance of dwellings, expansion of the concern's agricultural holdings, crèches and kindergartens, the equipment of rest-homes and sanatoria, dining-rooms, club premises, sports grounds, etc. as well as for giving individual bonuses to workers and employees, visits and stays at rest-homes and sanatoria, single assistance payments for wage-earners.

Prizes in socialistic competitions

Besides this, bonuses are paid out of the prize money presented to the winning concerns in the 'All-union Socialist Competition'. These prizes are financed by the concerns' profits or reductions in cost above those planned and they are allotted by the government. The amount of the prize-money varies with the size of the concern. In the foundry-industry, for example, the first prize in 1947 was 20,000 roubles for concerns with 100–250 workers and 700,000 roubles for concerns with over 30,000 workers.

Of the prize-money allotted to a concern in this competition 60 to 70 per cent has to go on individual bonuses and from 30 to 40 per cent on dwellings and other social and cultural welfare purposes. Of the amount allotted to individual bonuses, at least half must be used for rewarding the workers.

Special regulations on conditions of remuneration

There are special regulations concerning remuneration :— (1) of workers working several machines at the same time, or practising several crafts, (2) of clerks with dual-positions and lo-cumtenencies, (3) when work is interrupted or what is produced is not up to standard, (4) when working overtime, (5) when on night work, (6) when working on a holiday, (7) when absent from work on social or public business. Certain categories of workers and employees have special bonus-wages. The legislation also comprises regulations concerning the deductions that may be made from wages. The following is a brief account of these regu-lations, but it does not profess to be complete. *foot note* /

Stoppages and production of inferior goods

The regulations governing the remuneration to be paid during stoppages and when goods of inferior quality are being produced were issued in 1931 and 1932, and were intended to make the managements and workers of a concern directly interested in re-moving the causes of stoppages and the production of inferior goods.

Where work is interrupted, no wage is paid if the stoppage has been caused by the worker himself (*e.g.* if out of carelessness he has damaged a machine or a tool) or if he should have failed to have warned the management in time of anything which might cause a stoppage, or not at once have reported an incipient stop-page or have refused to allow himself to be transferred to other work because of the stoppage.

During a stoppage not caused by the worker, the worker is paid half or two-thirds of the time-rate in force for his tariff-class. If the stoppage occurs during a period when a new production is being started, then the full time-rate is paid. A management is obliged to take all measures to prevent a stoppage of work; if, however, a stoppage cannot be avoided, the workers affected are to be transferred to other work.

When a skilled worker or employee (from and including the fifth tariff-class) is transferred to lower qualified work because of a stoppage he is entitled to continue to receive his former average wage, provided he fulfils the norm for the work to which he has been transferred. If workers in the fifth or higher tariff-class do not fulfil the norms for their new work, or if they have been put on to work for which there is a time-rate, then they may retain the tariff-wage for workers on time-rates in the tariff-class to which they belonged previously.

Workers in the first four tariff-classes who are put on to lower-paid work because of a stoppage merely receive the wage of the work they actually do.

Where the transfer to lower-paid work has been made for reasons other than that of a stoppage, the employee or worker, whatever his tariff-class, retains his average wage earned at his previous work.

Wage-earners transferred to higher-paid work are paid according to the work they are doing.

Where, owing to the fault of the worker, the products have become quite unserviceable, no wage is paid, and for products inferior in quality yet capable of being used, a maximum of half the tariff-wage is paid.

If it is not the fault of the worker that the products have become inferior, quite unserviceable goods would normally be paid for with two-thirds of the tariff-wage and sub-standard but usable goods on a reduced scale of piece-rates.

Remuneration for overtime

Overtime work is paid at a higher rate than work in normal time. In most branches of industry time-rate workers receive a bonus-wage of 50 per cent for the first two hours of overtime and of 100 per cent for all subsequent hours. Piece-rate workers receive, in addition to their wage at their fixed piece-rate, an increment of 50 per cent of the tariff-wage for time-rate workers in the same tariff class during the first two hours and of 100 per cent for all subsequent hours.

In building and lumbering and in certain concerns in the timber industry, workers and employees with time-norms for their work receive an overtime bonus of 25 per cent of the tariff-wage for time-rate workers (or the basic wage) for the first two hours and of 50 per cent for all subsequent hours. There are also a number of other cases which have special regulations governing the remuneration of overtime.

Wage for night- and shift-work

There is generally a higher wage for *night-work*, *i.e.* work performed between 22.00 and 06.00 hours.

In shift-work on time-rate each hour of night-work performed by a worker who has an eight-hour or a seven-hour day is reckoned as eight-sevenths of an hour of day-work, and by workers who have a six-hour day, as six-fifths of an hour of day-work. In shift-work on a piece-wage the extra paid is one-seventh and one-fifth respectively of the worker's tariff-wage.

For night work which is not divided into shifts, time-rate workers with a working-day of 8, 7 or 6 hours are paid respectively eight-sevenths, seven-sixths or six-fifths of an hour of day-work for every hour of night-work. Piece workers receive an addition to their piece-rate earnings of one-seventh, one-sixth and one-fifth of the tariff-wage respectively for each hour of night-work.

With certain categories of workers, among them those in the peat industry, the extra for night-work is already included in the tariff-wage. Employees with non-normed working periods receive no addition.

The usual compensation for work done on Sundays or holidays is time-off. There are cases when special compensation is allowed.

Workers and employees have their wages made up while they are absent from work on certain types of social and public business, such as taking part in the proceedings of a court or in a congress, conference or such-like, which has been arranged by state or union organ, a co-operative organization, the Communist party or the league of youth.

Special increments

As has already been mentioned, for certain groups of workers the wage received differs according to the geographical area in which they work. Special regulations have been issued granting special increments for work done in certain remote areas, for long service in one and the same place of work, for knowledge of foreign languages, etc.

An addition on a percentage basis on account of old age is allowed for certain workers, among them those in the coal industry, the metal industry, the chemical industry, shipping, the postal, telegraph and telephone services. Thus, for example, in the coal industry those working underground receive an age-increment which after 15 years' work amounts to 30 per cent of the tariff wage.

Deductions from wages

Amounts may be deducted from wages only in those cases provided for by law; in order to cover a debt owned by the wage-earner to the state, his employer (concern or institution) or a 'third person'.

Thus the employer deducts from wages for income tax and the tax on small families (cf. pp. 99 and 101) and for the payment of amounts subscribed to state loans (cf. p. 104).

Further, deductions may be made in order to repay advances or amounts paid out owing to an error in calculation, in order to compensate for damage done to the concern's property and for holidays that have not been earned (if the employee leaves his position before completing a working-year for which he has already enjoyed a holiday).

There are special regulations governing deductions made on behalf of a third party. In cases of impounding for maintenance grants or damages for misappropriation and embezzlement of public property the amount deducted must not exceed 50 per cent of the wage. Similarly it is generally the rule that the total of all deductions may not exceed 50 per cent of the wage; if the claims on the wage-earner exceed this amount, maintenance grants and certain other claims have priority over taxes.

When a worker or employee is condemned to corrective labour at his place of work, for example for truancy, the judgment of the court states what proportion of his wage (at the most 25 per cent) the management of the concern or institution is to deduct. This deduction is made from the whole earned income with the exception of remuneration for overtime, unrepeated bonuses not paid out of the 'wage funds', pensions and benefit received from the social insurance, benefit given on leaving and defrayment of journey expenses. The deduction for corrective-labour is made irrespective of the size of any other of the deductions mentioned here.

Example of wage awards

The following are some concrete examples of wage-awards for workers and employees taken from various books of reference and other sources. One and all refer to the period after the general increase of the lower wage-incomes which was decreed in September 1946 (*cf.* p. 54).

Locomotive workshops in Kolomna

According to the model contract for the locomotive workshops in Kolomna which we have already mentioned on p. 56, those working in the metallurgical division were to be paid in accordance with a scale having 12 tariff-classes; the basic wage for 8 working-hours was 10·80 roubles in the lowest, and 36 roubles in the highest, tariff-class.

For building-workers there was a tariff-scale with 7 classes and the following basic wages (in roubles per hour):

	Lowest tariff-class	Highest tariff-class
Actual building-workers:		
on piece-work	1·27	3·07
on time-rates	1·01	2·17
Metal-workers:		
on piece-work	1·32	3·25
on time-rates	1·04	2·30

From one handbook of the conditions of work and wages in the coal industry in the eastern parts of the Soviet Union I have taken the following wage-awards (in force on 1st January 1948) for different categories of workers and employees. It should be emphasized that according to the awards made in 1946 the wages for certain groups of workers and employees in the coal industry (among them those working underground) were to be higher in the eastern than in the western parts of the country (*cf.* p. 65).

Those engaged on coal-cutting and constructional work in the mine are paid by the day or by the month. For those paid by the day, the basic wage varies, according to the worker's position, between 14·33 roubles (unskilled labourers above ground, among others) and 48 roubles (for certain machine-minders, drillers and such.) Store-workers underground had a basic wage of 450 roubles a month. Auxiliary workers such as charwomen, stokers, odd-job men, watchmen, coachmen, stable-boys, etc. had a monthly wage of 310 to 360 roubles.

For the ' leading crafts ' among the miners, there were different scales of progressive piece-work rates. According to one of these scales, double piece-rates were paid for that part of the output between 80 and 100 per cent of the norm, and treble the rate for any output above 1 per cent over the norm; according to another scale, the piece-rates were increased by 50 per cent and 100 per cent respectively, when the output lay between 90 and 100 per cent, or over 100 per cent of the norm. In other cases, the piece-rates were not raised until the norm had been surpassed.

Certain workers, like electricians, blasters, winchmen, etc. receive a bonus that varies with the amount of coal won each month for the whole mine, in a given locality, etc. The bonus amounts to 40 per cent of the basic wage, when the month's plan is achieved, and a further 3 per cent for every one per cent by which the plan is exceeded. Workers on time-rates who work well and do not have other bonuses receive a bonus corresponding to 20 per cent of their basic wage when the planned monthly output is achieved, and a further 3 per cent for every one per cent by which the plan is exceeded.

Working foremen of gangs engaged on coal-cutting receive an additional 40 to 50 per cent for organizing and leading the work, when the gang fulfils its month's norms, and a further amount of up to 25 per cent if the gang exceeds the norms. The foremen of other gangs which work underground receive an additional 20 per cent when the norm is achieved, and a further amount not above 15 per cent, if the norm is exceeded. Foremen have, besides, the right to special bonuses if they train their workers individually or as a gang; and these bonuses are further increased if the trained workers exceed their norms.

Wages of mechanics

In the engineering shops of the coal industry the workers' wage-scale comprises eight tariff-classes. The basic wages are as follows (roubles per hour):

	Tariff-class:	
	1	8
On time-rate, 'cold' work ..	1r. 21·1	2r. 94
Piece-rate on 'cold' work and on time-rate on 'hot' work	1r. 29·1	3r. 14·3
On piece-rate on 'hot' work	1r. 39·1	3r. 50·3

Progressive piece-rates have to be adopted for certain mechanic's jobs. In calculating the increments, use is made of a 'starting base', which, when the norm given the work is a theoretical norm, either corresponds to the output-norm or, if this is exceeded, the level of production achieved; with work the norm for which is based on experience, the 'starting base' is the level of production achieved by a qualified worker in the tariff-class in question. All satisfactory production over and above the 'starting base' which has been fixed (at least 100 per cent of the output norm in force) is paid for with higher piece-rates according to the following scale:

	Per cent above the starting base	Per cent increase in piece-rate
Mechanics with theoretical norms ..	0–15	50
over	15	100
Work with norms based on experience	0–15	30
	15–30	50
over	30	100

Time-rate workers in workshops under certain conditions receive a bonus, the maximum amount of which varies with the different kinds of production-departments. Thus repairers and electrical fitters receive a maximum of 40 or 50 per cent additional wage for reducing such stoppages as are connected with their work. Greasers receive a maximum of 25–30 per cent additional wage for reducing stoppages, and for recovery of lubricants they receive a maximum of 60 to 75 per cent of the sum saved by their doing so. Supervisors can receive a bonus wage of up to 30 to 50 per cent for scrupulous supervision, and storekeepers from 25 to 30 per cent for exemplary book-keeping and having raw materials, tools, etc. on hand when they are required. Working-foremen in the production departments receive up to 4 to 5 per cent extra for every one per cent by which the month's plan is exceeded. Cleaners, unskilled labourers and auxiliary workers, who are not attached to a production department, receive up to 20 to 25 per cent extra for effective service rendered to the production workers.

Wages for building workers

The handbook contains a number of wage-scales for building workers in different districts. In the lowest of these scales the hourly wage for actual builders on time-rate varies between 0·99 roubles in the first and 2·09 roubles in the seventh tariff-class, and in the highest scale between 1·24 and 2·97 roubles. In the ' other ' localities, not specified, the same scale is adopted as that already given (on p. 56) from the model agreement for the locomotive workshops in Kolomna.

Progressive piece-rates are adopted in building- and construction-work.

Working foremen on building work receive as a reward for leadership a wage-increment of 20 to 25 per cent of what they make by piece-work. In addition, they receive bonuses if the work is completed before the time fixed or if the number of men engaged on it is reduced from that envisaged in the plan.

Wages for builder's materials workers

In the coal industry's undertaking for the production of builder's materials (bricks, stone, asphalt, cement, etc.) there are seven classes in the tariff scales for workers. The workers are divided into three categories: (1) piece-workers in the leading crafts, engaged on hot, noxious and strenuous work; (2) piece-workers in the main- and auxiliary departments engaged on cold work, and time-rate workers in the leading crafts engaged on hot and noxious work; (3) other time-rate workers. The handbook gives tariff-scales for three different zones, showing the following basic wages (roubles per day):

	Zone 1: Tariff-class		Zone 2: Tariff-class		Zone 3: Tariff-class	
	1	7	1	7	1	7
Category 1 ..	10·57	23·51	10·09	22·37	9·61	20·84
„ 2 ..	9·85	21·60	9·43	20·26	9·00	18·88
„ 3 ..	9·13	19·30	8·78	18·18	8·39	16·93

For builder's materials workers there are two different scales for progressive piece-rates. According to one scale the piece-rates for that part of the production over and above the norm are to be raised by 50 or 100 per cent, if the norm is exceeded 1 to 10 or more than 10 per cent respectively; according to the other scale there is a corresponding increase when the norm is exceeded by from 1 to 20 and by more than 20 per cent. Time-rate workers, such as mechanics, electric fitters, greasers, etc. receive bonuses for the same reasons as workers in engineering workshops (*cf.* pp. 69–70).

Wages for Drivers

The handbook also gives the awards for fixed monthly wages and various kinds of bonuses for drivers, those loading lorries, and bus-drivers. The following are the basic wages (roubles per month) for the first zone, to which belong all localities in RSFSR with the exception of Moscow, Leningrad and certain remote districts in the second zone (Moscow and Leningrad) and in the third zone, which includes certain districts in the north and east, etc. A denotes work done on piece-rates, T work done on time-rate.

	Zone 1: A	T	Zone 2: A	T	Zone 3: A	T
Lorry-drivers, third class. Lorries with a load of:						
Up to 2·5 tons ..	410	380	430	407	460	424
2·5 – 5 tons ..	450	415	485	446·50	520	478
5 – 8 „ ..	500	460	540	496	580	532
8 – 10 „ ..	550	505	595	545·50	630	586
10 tons	615	565	667·50	601·50	720	648

	Zone 1:		Zone 2:		Zone 3:	
	A	T	A	T	A	T
Passenger vehicle drivers, third class.						
Vehicles with maximum of:						
5 seats	410	410	430	430	460	460
6 seats or more ..	450	450	485	485	520	520
Bus-drivers, second class:						
Up to 20 seats	540	500	584	540	618	580
20–32 ,, ...	600	550	640	595	690	630
32 seats or more ..	640	600	695	640	750	690
Lorry-loaders, all types of lorry	330	310	352	330	374	350
Bus-conductors:						
Up to 20 seats	—	285	—	302·50	—	320
20–32 ,, ...	—	310	—	330	—	350
32 seats or more ..	—	335	—	357·50	—	380

Drivers in the 1st and 2nd classes have respectively 35 and 15 per cent higher basic wages than drivers in 3rd class. Bus-drivers in the 1st class have 20 per cent higher basic wage than those in the 2nd class.

Piece-rates are worked out for lorry-drivers with a ' starting base ' of basic wages and norms; these take into account the size of the load and the number of kilometres driven. In certain cases progressive piece-rates have been adopted.

Special bonus payments are made for work on 'special vehicles' and lorries with trailers, *e.g.* 30 per cent (of the piece-wage or time-wage) for producer-gas lorries, 20 per cent for trailers with one axle, etc.

For drivers of passenger vehicles a ' non-normed working day ' can be adopted and this can carry a bonus corresponding to 25 to 50 per cent of the month's wage for ' systematically exceeding the hours of work '.

Drivers receive a bonus for saving petrol and tyres corresponding to 65 per cent of the sum saved in relation to the consumption planned. Further, bonuses are paid for driving without a summons, for exceeding the prescribed number of ton-kilometres and for reducing the need for repairs.

Wages in the coal industry

The following particulars concerning basic wages (in roubles per month) for heads of concerns, technicians, office personnel and others with monthly salaries, are taken from the handbook for the coal industry in the eastern areas.

Basic wage
(roubles per month)

Coal Mines

Heads and head engineers	1,800 to 3,000
Head engineer's assistant	1,320 „ 2,160
Head ventilation engineer	1,200 „ 2,160
Mine geologist	1,200 „ 1,440
First norm-er and planning engineer	960 „ 1,560
Norm-ers and economists	920 „ 1,080
Time-study men	550 „ 960
Foreman in electro-mechanical work-shop	690 „ 880
Head book-keeper	1,000 „ 1,500
First book-keeper	790 „ 980
First statistician	550 „ 690
Statisticians	500 „ 550
Superintendent of lodgings	500 „ 690

Factories and installations for coal concentration

Director, chief engineer	1,800 to 2,400
Head of department, concentration factory	1,080 „ 1,320
Foreman and department mechanic	800 „ 960
Head of chemical laboratory	980 „ 1,100
First laboratory worker	600 „ 790
Laboratory worker	500 „ 600

Power station (minimum 300 kilowatts)

Director, chief engineer	1,300 to 1,500
Heads of departments	790 „ 1,100
First departmental engineer	740 „ 980

Basic wage
(roubles per month)

Power station (minimum 300 kilowatts)

Departmental engineer	690 „	880
First departmental technician ..	600 „	740
Departmental technician	525 „	600
Repairs engineer	740 „	880
Norming engineer	640 „	740
First norming technician	550 „	690
Economist	550 „	640
Head book-keeper	880 „	1,000
First book-keeper	600 „	830
Book-keeper	500 „	690
First statistician	450 „	600
Cleaners, stokers, odd-job men, watch-men, coachmen, stable-lads, etc. ..	280 „	320

Scientific Research Institutions

Director of Institute	2,000 to	2,500
First scientist	1,250 „	1,500
Scientist	880 „	1,100
Laboratory-worker, First	790 „	830
Laboratory worker, draughtsman ..	600 „	690
Head of workshop	1,000 „	1,250
Foreman	790 „	980
Preparator, copyist	450 „	550
Stock-keeper	550 „	690
Photographer	690	
Cashier	450 „	550
Secretaries, typists	410 „	550
Director having title of professor or holding doctor's degree	6,000	
Head of laboratory with title of professor or holding doctor's degree ..	4,000	

Heads of concerns, technical personnel, supervisors of labour, etc. receive bonuses when the planned production and self-costs are achieved or bettered. In this, different methods are adopted for different groups of undertaking. Thus, for example, heads and head engineers of coal mines belonging to the 1st group of undertakings receive: (a) bonuses equivalent to not more than 100 per cent of their basic wage if the production plan is achieved, and further (b) at most 10 per cent for each one per cent by which the plan is exceeded. The corresponding maximum additions for certain other categories are given below:

	(a)	(b)
Mining concern, 2nd group:		
heads, head engineer	50	5
foremen in electro-mechanical shops	40	5
Briquette factories, 2nd group:		
directors, head engineers	50	5
first normer	30	3
Engineering workshops, 3rd group:		
directors, chief engineers	30	3
departmental heads, heads of laboratories, foremen	20	2

Further bonuses are given in the coal industry to the executive and technical staff for such reasons as reduction in self-costs, lowering of the ash-percentage, etc. The total of all bonuses (apart from prizes in the all-union socialist competition) may not exceed 300 per cent of the month's wage in mines and coal-concentration concerns, or 200 per cent in other concerns.

Wages in municipal undertakings

In 1948 the following basic wages (in roubles per day) were in force for workers in municipal undertakings in RSFSR:

Generating-stations and power-lines	Tariff-class:		
	1st	7th	8th
Piece-workers on cold and time-workers on hot work ..	9·93	19·11	21·86
Piece-workers on hot work ..	10·73	21·28	24·02
Time-workers on cold work ..	9·61	18·25	20·84

Tramways and rail-bus concerns (other than in Moscow and Leningrad)

	Tariff-class	
	1st.	7th.
Piece-workers on cold, and time-workers on hot work ..	10·73	23·14
Piece-workers on hot work ..	11·69	25·62
Time-workers on cold work ..	10·09	21·22

Water-supply and drainage

Piece-workers ..	..	8·31	15·89
Time-workers ..	..	7·90	15·03

In the state retail concerns and in the public places of refreshment, wages are differentiated according to the various geographical zones and type of undertaking.

Wages in retail establishments

The following account of the state of wages in state retail establishments is based on a handbook published in 1948. Since 1st March 1950 certain changes have taken place, in that bonuses of different kinds are now everywhere calculated with the planned sales as the starting-point (in accordance with *Planovoye Khozaistvo* 1950 : 2).

The sales-places coming under the Ministry of Trade are divided into five groups, those ' outside zone ' and zones 1, 2, 3 and 4. In concerns ' outside zone ' the basic wages are 20 per cent higher than in zone 1. The difference in wages between zones 1 and 4 ranges ' up to 20 per cent '.

The wages for managers of shops, departmental managers, foremen, sales-people, cashiers, and inspectors in many categories vary in accordance with the range of goods sold. Managers of shops, departmental managers, cashiers, etc. receive a bonus when the planned sales for the shop or department have been exceeded. Sales-people are on progressive piece-wages, the piece-rates being calculated from a starting-point, which for the individual is a ' handicap-norm ', for a department or entire shop the planned sales; piece-rates are raised by 50 per cent for that part of the turnover in excess of the norm, or plan. All categories mentioned in the following list are guaranteed 90 per cent of their basic wage even if the sales-plan is not achieved. Labourers and cleaners have a fixed basic wage and can receive in addition a bonus of 20 to 30 per cent of their monthly wage for ' qualitatively good work '.

These basic wages (in roubles per month) taken from the hand-book are for a ' mixed ' food store in Moscow (1st zone) with a planned turnover of 826,000 roubles a month (1948):

Director of the store	700
Vice-director of the store	630
Head of grocery department	600
Head of delicatessen department	630
Vice-head of grocery department	500
Vice-head of delicatessen department ..	530
Book-keeper	600
Labourer	300
Cleaner, woman	260
Sales-staff in grocery department:	
first salesman	370
salesman 1st class	330
„ 2nd „	290
Sales-staff in delicatessen department:	
first salesman	400
salesman 1st class	350
„ 2nd „	310
Cashier	340
Apprentice in delicatessen department ..	210

Wages in places of public refreshment

In places of public refreshment (restaurants, buffets, tearooms, etc.) the principles by which wages are fixed are, according to Maximenko's textbook *The Economy and Planning of Public Places of Refreshment* (published 1949), the same as for the retail trades. Those in charge and the administrative staff either have a fixed basic wage with additional increments or a wage that varies with the turnover of the undertaking or individual department. Various forms of piece-wages are adopted for kitchen staff and serving staff. If the production norms are fulfilled, additional bonuses of up to 20 per cent of the basic wage are paid to the kitchen staff for preparing food of good quality, to the serving staff for good service to customers, and to washers-up for a ' qualitatively' good result of their work. Special bonuses are paid for reducing the loss of weight in the cleaning of vegetables, etc.

The executive staff, the kitchen staff and several other categories have a guaranteed minimum wage corresponding to 85 per cent of their wage basic even if they do not fulfil the plan or norm.

The following examples of basic wages in an undertaking with 32 employees are taken from Maximenko.

Wage per month (roubles)

Head of production	830
Head of dining-room	880
Book-keeper	550
Calculator	400
Cloakroom attendant	260
Watchman	260

Wage per day (roubles)

Tariff-class 1: auxiliary worker, dining-room cleaner	9·21
„ 2: kitchen cleaner, washer-up	9·77
„ 3: waitress	10·41
„ 4: cashier, assistant to cook	11·37
„ 5: cook (3rd category)	12·65
„ 6: „ (2nd „)	14·57
„ 7: „ (1st „) confectioner ..	17·62

Wages for teachers

Finally, some example should be given of the wages fixed for school- and college-teachers.

Teachers' wages are graduated according to both locality (town and urban community, or country) and to length of service. After 25 years' service teachers are entitled to a pension, which they receive in full even if they remain in service. In the country districts and in urban communities teachers have free quarters.

The following table gives the basic wages, in roubles per month, of certain categories of teachers in RSFSR as they were fixed on 1st February 1948.

	Town workers' communities			Country		
	Teaching service, years:			Teaching service, years:		
	Up to 5	5–10	Over 10	Up to 5	5–10	Over 10
Teachers in classes 1 to 4 with:						
1. Training at pedagogic middle school	575	635	690	520	575	635
2. Training at general middle school	520	575	635	490	545	605
Teachers of mother tongue, literature, mathematics, history, languages, etc. :						
in classes 5 to 7 with:						
1. College training	690	735	795	635	690	735
2. Training in teachers' institute	660	710	765	605	660	710
in classes 8 to 10:						
1. With college training	710	765	850	660	710	765
2. Without completed training at college	690	735	795	635	690	735

These basic wages are for four hours' teaching per day in classes 1 to 4, and in classes 5 to 10 three hours per day. With more hours' teaching, the wage is raised in proportion. Special additional bonuses are paid for class superintendents, for the correction of exercises, etc., and in certain districts there is a location-bonus.

In March 1946 regulations were issued increasing the wages of the academic staffs of research institutes and for professors and teachers at the higher educational establishments. At the higher medical schools basic wages varied, according to training, seniority and position in the service, from 2,800 to 6,000 roubles a month for professors, from 2,000 to 3,000 roubles for lecturers and from 1,750 to 2,700 roubles for demonstrators and other college teachers. The basic wage for the rector of a higher educational establishment was 4,000 to 8,000 roubles per month.

Wage-level according to the Five-year Plan

According to the Five-year Plan for 1946–1950 the 'average year's wage' for workers and employees in 1950 was to have reached 6,000 roubles. If the amount of the 'wages fund for workers and employees' given in the plan (252·3 milliard roubles) is divided by the planned number of workers and employees (33·5 million) it gives the sum of 7,531 roubles. Since the plan was adopted, the 'dear-times increment' mentioned on p. 54 was added to wages in September 1946. An almanack published in 1949 (1950 *Kalendar-spravochnik*) mentions that the wages of certain categories of employees in Ural, Siberia and the Far East were raised by 20 per cent in August 1946, and that wages for teachers were increased in 1948. No statistics of average incomes for the last few years have been available.

CHAPTER VI

WORKERS' PROTECTION

THIS chapter is devoted partly to the regulations concerning safety-measures and sanitary conditions in places of work, and partly to certain special regulations about conditions of work for women and young persons.

General and special regulations for the protection of workers

All concerns and institutions are obliged to adopt measures to prevent accidents and injury whilst working, and to keep places of work in a hygienic state in accordance with the instructions issued by the authorities or trade union organization. Certain regulations concerning safety measures, factory-sanitation, etc. that apply to industrial life as a whole are put out by the Council of Ministers, while special regulations for the different branches are prepared by the central committees of the trade unions in question in conjunction with the interested authorities.

Inspection of new concerns

Before work is started in a newly built or freshly equipped concern it must be inspected to see that it will give workers the requisite protection. The inspection is made by a commission, one member of which is a technical inspector from the trade union concerned.

As a rule the yearly production- and finance-plan of a concern contains a special allocation for measures to improve workers' protection and factory-hygiene, such as safety measures, ventilation, etc. The actual details of how the allocation is to be used may be a matter for agreement between the management and the local union organization; such agreements are added as supplements to the collective agreements for the different places of work.

Means of protection

In the case of all noxious work and in certain other cases as well, *e.g.* work done in abnormal temperatures—the workers should have ' special clothing ' and ' special shoes ', which are issued either against payment or gratis, as well as the requisite means of protection (spectacles, gloves, gas-masks, etc.), which belong to the concern and are issued free. In certain cases 'special soap', antidotes (*e.g.* milk), etc. are supplied free.

Medical examination

Certain employees should have a medical examination before taking up employment. Among such are workers under 18 years of age and workers who are to be employed on heavy work or on noxious matter (*e.g.* lead and arsenic). In certain cases periodical medical examination is enjoined.

Accidents during work

All accidents occurring to workers and employees in connection with their work in production must be registered if they have led to loss of ability to work for at least one working day; in every case of such accident the head of the department concerned must within 24 hours investigate its cause and draw up a report according to a certain fixed formula. All accidents which have caused loss of ability to work for more than three days shall be reported also to the management and to the superior economic and trade organ.

Work of women and minors

According to the labour code it is as a rule not permitted to employ persons under the age of 16 as wage-earners. This minimum age can, however, be reduced to 14 in special cases on receipt of permission from the union organization. Young persons between the age of 14 and 16 have a shorter normal working day (*cf.* p. 48).

Women and persons under 18 are not allowed to be employed on certain heavy and unhealthy work. Certain maxima have been fixed for the weights that may be lifted, carried or wheeled by women and minors.

Young persons under 16 and nursing mothers are not allowed to do night work or overtime. Pregnant women are not allowed to do night work, nor, from the fifth month of pregnancy, overtime.

Should the need arise, pregnant women are to be transferred to lighter work while retaining the average wage they have earned during the previous six months (*cf.* p. 43). For the 35 calendar days prior to and the 42 days after childbed, women workers and employees are entitled to be absent from work and are then in receipt of assistance from the social insurance, if they have been in the same concern for an unbroken period of at least three months. In the event of an abnormal birth or the birth of twins the period of free time after childbed is prolonged to 56 days. Concerns and institutions are obliged to give pregnant women their ordinary holidays in addition to the absence permitted because of pregnancy.

Nursing mothers are entitled to ' suckling-pauses ' in addition to the ordinary rests. The maximum interval between these suckling-pauses is $3\frac{1}{2}$ hours, and, in contrast to the intervals for meals, they are reckoned as working-time and paid for in accordance with the women's average earnings.

Inspection of protective measures

As has already been mentioned, the duties of the former Labour Commissariat were transferred in 1933 to the All-Union Council. At the same time, the control of workers' protection was transferred to the trade unions. This control is organized at branch-level within the different trade unions and is directed by the All-Union Council.

In each local trade union organization 'social inspectors' or commissions for workers' protection are appointed, and these co-operate in the working-out of plans and the implementation of measures in this sphere and superintend the application of the laws and instructions concerning safety measures, working hours, the employment of women and minors, etc.

The trade unions' committees for the provinces, districts, towns and regions have special commissions for workers' protection. The work of the local and regional organs is directed by the unions' central committee, which has a department for these matters. The person in charge of this department is that central committee's technical inspector, who must have technical training and be familiar with conditions in the branch.

The technical inspector has to see to the safety of workers in those concerns and institutions whose personnel come under his union. He must (a) make regular visits to the concerns and institutions he has to supervise and see that they are complying with the regulations, rules and norms concerning safety measures and factory hygiene; (b) take measures to remove infringements or defects he may notice in this sphere; (c) see that steps are taken to improve working conditions and to assist in the prevention of accidents and occupational sickness.

The technical inspector has the right at any time to go over a concern, to demand explanations from the management, to issue compulsory instructions to stop infringements of rules or norms, to initiate investigations of offences against the safety regulations, to inflict fines, to give orders (through the director or person in charge of the building) for work to be stopped at a place of work where there is immediate danger to the lives or health of the workers, to take part in commissions inspecting new erections and reconstructed concerns, etc.

Besides these organs for the supervision of workers' protection, which come under the trade unions, there are a number of special state organs of inspection, *inter alia* the sanitary inspectorate of the Ministry of Health, and the technical inspectorate of mines.

CHAPTER VII

LABOUR DISCIPLINE

THE following declarations of principle are taken from a text-book, *The Labour Laws of the Soviet Union*:

' In the socialistic community labour discipline is mainly safe-guarded by the method of convincing the majority of workers of the necessity to observe discipline in their work. In this connection the socialist state awards various rewards for conscientious work and for outstanding achievement in work.

' But towards the minority, the unenlightened and backward workers who in their attitude to work have not yet overcome the residue of capitalism—towards them, where the case demands it, means of compulsion are used to see that they observe discipline in their work.'

In another connection the book mentions a number of the measures taken, among others in the sphere of wage-policy, social insurance and housing, to stimulate wage-earners to work efficiently and with discipline and to stay longer at one place-of-work. Here, in this chapter, I shall give some account of these special regulations concerning labour discipline and the consequences of its neglect.

Wage-earners' responsibility for infringements of discipline

For the different categories of workers and employees there are different kinds of disciplinary rules, technical regulations and service instructions, which contain more detailed provisions concerning the duties and obligations of the wage-earner. In cases of neglect of labour discipline the management may adjudge disciplinary punishment. Certain infringements of labour discipline involve judicial proceedings. Besides this ' disciplinary ' or ' criminal ' liability, employees have ' material responsibility ' (liability for damages) in cases of infringement of discipline that causes the concern or institution material damage.

The internal ordering of work in concerns and institutions is regulated partly through 'rules for the internal ordering of work' or disciplinary rules, partly through technical directions, service instructions, etc.

Rules for the internal ordering of work

On 18th January 1941 the Government laid down 'model rules for the internal ordering of the work of workers and employees in State, co-operative and social concerns and institutions', which had been worked out by the All-Union Council. At the same time, it was directed that the People's Commissariats (nowadays ministries) should issue special rules, based on these model rules, for the various branches, and this they were to do in conjunction with the central committees of the various trade unions, any necessary complementary rules required for special cases being worked out by the director or head of the place of work in conjunction with the local trade union organization.

These model rules embody regulations concerning the procedure for recruiting and dismissing workers and employees, the basic duties of management, workers and employees, the period of work and its exploitation, and punishment for infringements of discipline plus certain references to relative legislation.

According to these model rules a management is bound to organize work in such a way that each worker and employee is employed in accordance with his speciality and qualification. Further, it is incumbent upon the management at the right time to issue orders about the work and to provide the workers with tools, material and spare parts, to see that the machinery, workbenches and such-like are in good order, to give each worker and employee a definite place in which to work, machine, etc., to enhance labour discipline, raise productivity and introduce Stakhanovite methods into their work.

The obligations of workers and employees are to work honestly and conscientiously, to observe discipline in work, to carry out the orders of the management swiftly and exactly, to observe the time for work strictly and without evasion, to fulfil the output norms and give qualitatively good results in their work, to look

86

after socially-owned property (machinery, work-benches, tools, raw materials, etc.).

There are special disciplinary rules for employees in transport and certain other branches. These embody, among other things, special regulations concerning disciplinary punishments and rewards for outstanding work.

The general regulations concerning the obligations of wage-earners embodied in the rules for the internal ordering of work are supplemented by detailed regulations in the technical directions and service instructions, etc.

Disciplinary punishment

The management of a concern or institution—or its superior authority or organization—can adjudge disciplinary punishment for such infringements of labour discipline as do not involve criminal liability. The rules for the internal ordering of work, like the disciplinary rules for many categories of railway personnel, embody directives on the different kinds of disciplinary punishments that may be adjudged in this way. For certain employees in responsible positions, selected functionaries, etc. there are special regulations concerning disciplinary responsibility.

All disciplinary punishments must be meted out within a limited time of the offence being committed or discovered. Before punishment is adjudged the wage-earner shall be afforded an opportunity of providing an explanation. It is possible to appeal against such disciplinary punishment, and a previously adjudged punishment may be revoked after a certain period of irreproachable work.

According to the model rules for the internal ordering of work, for infringements of discipline the management of a concern may adjudge one or other of the following punishments: bad mark, reprimand, severe reprimand, transfer to lower-paid work for a maximum of three months (for workers) or to a lower grade (for employees). If a wage-earner systematically infringes the rules for the internal ordering of work and the measures just mentioned have led to no improvement, he may be dismissed in accordance with the provisions of the labour code. Disciplinary punishments may not be inflicted if a month has elapsed since the offence was discovered. Appeals against them may be lodged with the conflict-commission (*cf.* Chapter VIII) or brought before the courts.

Those employed on the railways may, in accordance with the special regulations affecting them, have the following disciplinary punishment inflicted upon them: bad mark, reprimand, severe reprimand, arrest for a maximum of ten days while continuing to go on duty or without going on duty and without pay; transfer to other lower-paid work for three months at the most or to a lower grade, reduction in personal title. Such punishments may be appealed against to higher authority.

Liability for arbitrary departure and truancy

The penal code contains regulations for the punishment of certain kinds of violation of labour discipline, among them 'arbitrary departure' (*samovolny ukhod*) and 'truancy' (*progul*).

In accordance with the ukase of 26th June 1940 (see pp. 18–19), the punishment for arbitrary departure from work in a state, co-operative or social enterprise or institution by worker or employee is 2 to 4 months' imprisonment, and for truancy without valid reason corrective labour at the place of work for a maximum of 6 months and deduction from wage not exceeding 25 per cent.

According to the model rules for the internal ordering of work, it shall be regarded as truancy if a wage-earner arrives late for the beginning of the working day or after a meal-interval, or if he leaves work before the end of his working day or before the beginning of the meal-interval, in so far as this leads to more than 20 minutes of working time being lost. Absence from work for a shorter period than 20 minutes is also counted as truancy if it is repeated on three occasions in one month or four times in two successive months. It is also regarded as truancy for a worker or employee to be not sober at work.

It is stated in *The Labour Laws of the Soviet Union* that the decisions of the supreme court have led to exacter definition of the ' valid reasons ' for absence from work which absolve the person concerned from being punished for truancy, thus, for example, a wage-earner is not responsible for lateness caused by communications not keeping to the time-table. According to a judgment of the supreme court in 1943 which is discussed in

Labour Legislation, it shall be accounted sufficient reason for absence if a wage-earner has in good faith attended a doctor for treatment of sickness, even though the doctor did not issue a certificate of illness.

It is considered ' arbitrary departure ' if a wage-earner leaves his employment without permission of the management. As was explained in Chapter 3 there are certain cases where the management is bound to give its permission. The same penalty as for ' arbitrary departure ' is inflicted in the following cases: (1) when a wage-earner has not obeyed a request to move to another place of work which is issued based on the ukase of 19th October 1940 (*cf*. p. 18); (2) when a wage-earner has infringed the rules for the internal ordering of work with the aim of being dismissed; (3) when a wage-earner is truant without valid reason for the third time during a period of performing corrective labour at his place of work because of previous repeated truancy.

In *The Penal Code of the Soviet Union* (published 1950) an account is given of a ' guiding decree ' from the supreme court of the Soviet Union dated 22nd October 1942, in which it was declared that if a wage-earner remains absent from work over a long period of time, that can only be regarded as truancy if the court decides that his absence was not actuated by the intention to leave his work at the concern or institution in question.

If ' specialists ' who have gone through a trade middle school, college or post-graduate college (*aspirantur*) do not report to the employment to which they were directed by the competent ministry or authority (*cf*. p. 45), they are punished as for ' arbitrary departure ' or ' truancy '.

Besides ' arbitrary departure ' and ' truancy ' there are, according to the penal code, certain specially grave infringements of labour discipline committed by wage-earners in transport and production-departments where there is risk of explosion, etc. which are dealt with by the courts.

Liability for damages

The Labour Laws contain provisions relating to the liability of wage-earners to make good damage caused by them to the enterprise or institution where they are working (' material liability'). In certain cases this liability for damages may be limited to a maximum sum which has a certain relationship to the wage of the person involved: in other cases the damages have to cover or exceed the value of the loss inflicted. Damages shall not be exacted in those cases where the damage or loss can be attributed to ' normal production-economic risks '.

Workers and employees must make compensation in full for damage and loss caused to their enterprise or institution in the execution of their tasks, if the damage has been caused through a criminal act, or if full liability for damages is specially decreed or agreed. In all such cases, disputes as to the extent of the compensation shall be laid before a court.

Compensation for more than the value is exacted in the case of raw materials, semi-manufactured and finished products (in certain cases), in respect of special clothing, protective appliances, tools and such-like that are loaned to the wage-earner. If a wage-earner purloins or deliberately destroys or damages such objects, he must pay five times the value of the loss involved. If an object has been lost through carelessness, or if special clothing, tools, etc. loaned to him are damaged through carelessness, the wage-earner shall pay at the most five times the value of the loss. In such cases the damages are to be deducted from the wage-earner's wages or other remuneration which is owed by the concern (*e.g.* ' departure benefit', holiday compensation, etc.). A management's decision to make such deductions may be appealed against to the conflict commission (see p. 51). On each occasion when payment is made, these deductions may not exceed 25 per cent and in conjunction with other deductions not more than 50 per cent of the wage and other remuneration due to the wage-earner (*cf.* p.66). Liability for enhanced damages is exacted also in cases concerning certain domestic animals and certain kinds of fuel.

Liability is limited in cases where full or increased compensation is not decreed. Thus, maximum damages of one-third of the wage-earner's basic monthly wage are inflicted for certain losses caused by carelessness in work involving infringement of existing laws, of rules for internal ordering of work, or of special instructions and directions issued by the management, in so far as there is no criminal liability. This is the case, among other things, with damage, destruction or loss of means of production (machinery, apparatus) and other property, with the exception of raw materials, semi-manufactured goods and finished products and special clothing, tools, etc. loaned to the wage-earner. In other cases, the maximum of damages is fixed at higher amounts, for example at a maximum of two-thirds of the monthly wage if damage is done to raw materials, semi-manufactures and finished products through carelessness.

CHAPTER VIII

Labour Conflicts

The concept ' Labour Conflict '

ACCORDING to *The Labour Laws of the Soviet Union*, the term ' labour conflict ' (*trudovoi spor*) means a dispute between wage-earner and the management of a concern or institution over ' the establishing or putting into practice of rights or obligations concerned with the work '. The parties in such a dispute are on the one side a worker or employee or a group of workers or employees, and on the other side the management of a concern or of an institution. The organ of the trade union (factory committee, provincial committee, etc.) can take part in a labour conflict as representative of the workers and employees.

Different kinds of labour conflict

Labour conflicts in this meaning of the term may arise either in connection with the introduction of new regulations concerning conditions of work, or out of the application of stipulations in labour contracts or legislation.

The former type of dispute is concerned with questions that have not been completely regularized by legislation and which are decided either through collective agreement, by arrangement between the management of the concern and the wage-earner or trade union organization, or by means of such measures on the part of the management as presuppose the consent of the trade union organization.

In such disputes as concern the application of regulations in force, the party who considers his right infringed can claim steps to obtain rectification. The following are examples of this kind of dispute: (1) a wage-earner claims remuneration for work done or challenges the concern's right to dismiss him and claims compensation for enforced idleness; (2) the manager of an enterprise demands that a wage-earner should be ordered to make compensation for damage he has caused to the enterprise.

Dealing with labour conflicts

Labour conflicts can be resolved (1) by arrangement between the representatives of the parties on the conflict commission, (2) by a decision of the court, or (3) by decision of a superior authority.

The local organ for resolving labour conflicts is ' the piece-rate and conflict commission ' (RKK), which for the sake of brevity will be referred to as the ' conflict commission '.

The conflict commission must consist of equal numbers of representatives of the management of the enterprise and the local union organization (factory-, workshop-, or house-committee, group-committee, or regional committee). It deals with conflicts that arise between wage-earner and employer over the application of legislation, labour contract and internal rules. Such conflicts can be referred either to the conflict commission or to the people's court.

Besides this, the conflict commission has the duty of dealing with disputes concerning the introduction or alteration of working conditions that cannot be regularized directly through legislation and other ' normative acts ', and with certain questions concerning holidays.

According to the regulations drawn up in 1928, the conflict commissions have to deal with a large number of questions concerning the fixing and altering of working conditions, including output-norms and piece-rates: the competence of the commissions in this latter respect has been considerably restricted since that date. According to the directive issued in 1933 by the All-Union Council, performance-norms and piece-rates are to be fixed by the management of the enterprise (cf. pp. 32 and 57); individual workers and trade union organs could, however, submit protests against such decisions to the conflict commission. The system in force in 1949 has been summarized by two writers as follows:

'The conflict commission can deal with complaints of faulty application of performance-norms, piece-rates and tariff-wage rates, but not conflicts concerned with their introduction.' (*The Labour Laws of the Soviet Union.*) 'The conflict commissions deal with questions of performance-norms and piece-rates only in the event of their rightness being in dispute.' (Pasherstnik.) No further details of the regulations and practice in this connection have been obtainable.

The conflict commission is perforce the court of first instance for conflicts concerned with the following questions: transfer to other work and retention of wage in connection with the transfer; payment when the norm has not been fulfilled and payment for goods of inferior quality; dismissal on grounds of incompetence or dereliction of duty (with certain exceptions); compensation for the use of tools belonging to the wage-earner; the issue of special clothing and special food or monetary compensation in lieu; the application of regulations concerning reductions in working-time and extension of holidays; payment for acting as substitute on work of a different qualification than the customary; payment during stoppages of work; payment when preparing for piece-work; payment for piece-work uncompleted; deduction from wages of damages caused by the wage-earner to the concern (with certain exceptions); payment for time when the wage-earner was kept away from his work; payment of monetary compensation for holidays not granted; payment during the trial period of a newly engaged wage-earner; the amount of bonuses allotted to the wage-earner; payment for overtime; meeting a wage-earner's vital requirements in cases where the management of the enterprise does not fulfil its contractual engagements.

In other conflicts than those mentioned above, *e.g.* in the event of dismissal due to reduction in personnel, the wage-earner is free to choose whether to lay it before the conflict commission or to take it to court.

The conflict commission does not deal with certain conflicts the resolving of which requires the decision of an authority (*e.g.* conflicts over the dismissal of certain wage-earners in specially responsible positions, concerning certain kinds of disciplinary punishment or of dismissal at the request of a trade union organization). Also outside the commission's competence are matters concerning the alteration of employees' wages that have been fixed by state norming, or 'personal wages' (*cf.* p. 61), the fixing or altering of establishments, matters that have been decided or been dealt with by a court, conflicts concerning workers and employees in a concern where no employees are members of a trade union.

In the larger concerns separate conflict commissions may be set up for the different departments.

When a dispute over the application of current regulations concerning working conditions is laid before the conflict commission, it can be settled by arrangement between the two parties' representatives on the commission. If agreement is not reached in the commission, either party can refer the dispute to the popular court.

A wage-earner or management of a concern may appeal against the decision of a conflict commission to the superior organ of the trade union concerned (*e.g.* provincial committee, district committee or central committee), as the trade unions have had the duty of supervising the activities of the conflict commissions since 1933, when the People's Commissariat for Labour was merged with the All-Union Council (*cf.* p. 16). This organ can rescind the decision of a conflict commission in the following cases:

If working-conditions have been rendered worse than those laid down by law or labour contract; if the maximum norms fixed by law or contract have been exceeded; if there has been an infringement of the rules governing the organization, competence and procedure of the conflict-commission and this could have influenced the decision; if the decision was based on false documents or erroneous information; if circumstances come to light which were not known to the conflict commission when the matter was decided and which are of essential importance for a proper solution of the question; if the conflict commission made a decision on a matter which had already been settled or dealt with by a court of law.

If a superior trade union organ rescinds the decision of a conflict commission, the matter in dispute can either be dealt with afresh by the commission or be referred to the popular court. Popular courts also deal with conflicts over the application of regulations in those cases where agreement could not be reached in the conflict commission, or where the conflict commission is not the obligatory first instance (*cf.* p. 94). The decision of a popular court may be appealed against to a higher instance (see p. 41).

CHAPTER IX

TAXES AND STATE LOANS

THE State budget of the Soviet Union comprises the incomes and expenditures of all the republics of the Union and of lesser administrative units, like provinces, regions, towns, etc. In the budget for 1949 the incomes and expenditures totalled respectively 446·0 and 415·4 milliard roubles, while the real incomes and expenditures for that year (1949) amounted to 437·0 and 412·3 milliard roubles respectively. In the budget for 1950 income was calculated at 433·2 and expenditure at 427·9 milliard roubles; the actual amounts being 422·1 and 412·7 milliard roubles. The 1951 budget which was accepted by the Supreme Soviet in March 1951 provided for an income of 458·7 milliard roubles and expenditure of 451·5 milliard roubles.

According to the 1949 budget the income was divided among the following main heads thus:

Income in 1949 budget

	Million roubles
Turn-over tax	262,168·0
Proceeds from State enterprises	29,592·8
Income from machinery- and tractor-stations	3,328·0
Income tax and other payments from concerns, economic organizations and institutions	10,427·8
Taxes from population	36,467·6
State loans	23,121·0
Social insurance funds	17,491·0
Customs and income from war-damages ..	22,441·7
Dues and various receipts, other than taxes	12,500·775
Re-valuation of stocks	13,153·0
Incomes of the autonomous republics and local soviets out of local sources ..	14,552·5
Balance from republic- and local-budgets	799·1

G

The major part of the State income comprised the proceeds of turn-over tax and other payments from State concerns and economic organizations (such as collective agriculture and co-operative handicraft organizations). Under the heading 'taxes from population' are lumped direct taxes, object-taxes and certain other charges which are levied on a personal basis. It is a heading that we shall discuss further along with 'State loans'.

The item 'taxes from population' increased from 35·8 milliard roubles in 1950 to 43·4 milliard in the budget for 1951, and the item 'State loans' from 31·0 to 33·4 milliard roubles. According to Minister of Finance Zverev's report on the 1951 budget, the increase in 'taxes from population' was due to the fact that an increase in 'the wage fund' (that is the planned wage total) for workers and employees was anticipated; besides they had reckoned on a restriction of certain reliefs of income tax for certain groups of the population. The following account of taxation legislation is based mainly on a handbook for taxation authorities published in 1950.

The taxes paid by the private individual are the agricultural tax (*selskokhoziastvenni nalog*), income tax (*podokhodny nalog*), as well as the taxes on those without dependants and those with small or no families (bachelor tax).

Agricultural tax

The agricultural tax is paid by collective farmers and individual peasants as well as by workers, clerks, artisans, etc. who receive income from agriculture in the country. The amount payable is fixed on the basis of the income per household and this is assessed in accordance with certain norms-of-yield; individual peasants are also taxed on their income from sales in the market. Collective-farmers pay agricultural tax only on their income from agricultural work done on their own account; besides this, the collective farm as such pays a separate tax.

Income tax

Income tax is paid by persons resident in towns and 'workers' communities', and also by those resident in the country who have an income from other sources than agriculture. It is fixed differently for different categories of taxpayer and for different sources of income. In the taxable income are not included gains and interest on State loans, savings-bank funds, etc., nor remuneration received from State insurance, State benefit for mothers with large families, amounts received through inheritance or as a gift,* pensions and certain other incomes.

Special reliefs of income tax have been prescribed for members of the armed forces, for those who have been decorated or granted titles of honour (Heroes of the Soviet Union and Heroes of Socialist Labour) or who have been awarded Stalin prizes, and for many kinds of inventors.

The income tax deducted from the earned income of workers and employees is, as a rule, as given in the following table and is paid by the wage-earner in periodic deductions from his wages, calculated on the income for the preceding month's work:

Income per month (roubles)	Tax per month						
151–200	.. 2·25 roubles	+	5·5% of income above 150 roubles				
201–300	.. 5 ,,	+	6%	,,	,,	,, 200	,,
301–400	.. 11 ,,	+	7%	,,	,,	,, 300	,,
401–500	.. 18 ,,	+	8%	,,	,,	,, 400	,,
501–700	.. 26 ,,	+	10%	,,	,,	,, 500	,,
701–1,000	.. 46 ,,	+	12%	,,	,,	,, 700	,,
1,001 and over	.. 82 ,,	+	13%	,,	,,	,, 1,000	,,

According to this scale, a person with a monthly income of 600 roubles has to pay in tax 26 roubles plus 10 per cent of 100 (600–500) roubles, that is, 26 + 10 = 36. For all incomes above 1,000 roubles the ' marginal ' income tax is 13 per cent.

In the taxable wages are included all income from wages, such as basic wage, remuneration for overtime and piece-work, personal bonus, such bonuses as are paid in accordance with the regulations on wage-bonuses, benefit from social insurance while temporarily unable to work, compensation for holidays not received, etc. On the other hand, tax is not paid on individual bonuses and rewards of a non-repetitive character which are paid as the management sees fit and which are not provided for in the regulations concerning the system of payment, nor is tax paid on travelling allowances and expenses, ' departure benefit ', compensation for tools, etc.

* A special stamp duty is payable for attestation of right to inherit (cf. p. 103).

At the place of work where the worker or employee has his main employment a wage-income of under 260 roubles a month is free of tax. Incomes from subsidiary occupations are not calculated in with the main income, but are taxed separately at each place of work; for these incomes there is no tax-free minimum allowed, but subsidiary incomes of less than 150 roubles a month are taxed at the rate of 1·5 per cent.

Where a worker or employee is liable for the maintenance of more than three persons, the tax on the income from his main occupation is reduced by 30 per cent.

The principles by which workers and employees are taxed on their wage-incomes are the same as those adopted in taxing the remuneration received by writers and artists for literary work, commissioned work, etc., as also the stipendia paid to students if they exceed 260 roubles a month. The above rates are applied with an increase of 10 per cent to artisans organized in a co-operative and for those working at home, who do not use their own raw materials.

Those who practise an independent trade, such as doctors, dentists, nurses, teachers, advocates, typists, etc. with private practices, pay taxes on the income from these activities on a more severe progressive scale. With a yearly income of not more than 1,800 roubles, the income tax is 2 per cent; with an income of from 1,801 to 2,400 roubles, it is 36 roubles plus 6 per cent of the amount in excess of 1,800 roubles, and so on. For yearly incomes above 70,000 roubles, the tax is 25,324 roubles plus 55 per cent of the amount in excess of 70,000 roubles. If one and the same person has both an income from a paid employment and from independent practice (private practice, etc.), the different incomes are taxed individually on the different scales.

A still higher scale is used in the taxation of private (not co-operatively organized) handicraft and certain other incomes that are not wages, *e.g.* income from work at home with one's own material or own equipment of a certain kind, income from agriculture in urban communities, income from renting-out buildings, apartments and rooms, priests' remuneration for conducting religious services, etc. For these incomes the tax is at 3 per cent if the income is not above 1,800, between 1,801 and 2,400 roubles it is 54 roubles plus 8 per cent of the amount by which the income exceeds 1,800 roubles, etc.; for yearly incomes over 70,000 roubles, the tax is 30,958 roubles plus 65 per cent of the amount in excess of 70,000 roubles.

'Bachelor tax'

The special tax on bachelors, lone persons and those with small or no families is paid by men between the ages of 20 and 50 and women between the ages of 20 and 45, who do not have children or who have one child or two children. It is even paid by those who do not have incomes of their own; yet certain categories are exempt, among them certain members of the armed forces, certain students under the age of 25, disabled persons in the first and second groups (cf. p. 116), women who are in receipt of assistance or pension for the maintenance of children, Soviet citizens whose children fell in the Second World War, etc.

Workers and employees pay in 'bachelor tax' 6 per cent of their wage if they have no children, and 1½ and 1 per cent respectively if they have one child, or two children. The same percentages apply to those paying the tax who are artisans, house-owners, persons engaged in agriculture in urban communities, and others with an income that is not wages. In these cases, the tax is calculated on the total annual income but must not be less than the amount charged against persons without an income of their own, i.e. 90, 30 and 15 roubles respectively for those with no, one or two children. The corresponding amounts for collective-farmers, independent peasants and others paying agricultural tax, are 150, 50 and 25 roubles a year respectively.

Other taxes and imposts

Of the other taxes and imposts paid by the people, mention must be made of the taxes and dues for income from fishing, the horse tax for independent peasants, 'self-taxation' in the country, certain local taxes and dues—for example building tax and 'ground rent', tax on means of transport and cattle, fee for the right to sell wares at the kolkhoz markets (cf. p. 103)—and the State stamp duties.

Self-taxation

' Self-taxation ' is resorted to in the country and in villa communities; it is a rate levied by decision of a general meeting of citizens in a village or community for certain local purposes, such as work on roads and bridges, the erection and repair of schoolhouses, the repair of hospitals, provision of equipment and premises for a fire-brigade, etc. There are certain maxima for the amounts that may be levied at any one time; for collective farmers, workers and employees and artisans organized in a co-operative the maximum is 20 roubles per household, for independent peasant households with cultivated land or working-beasts 75 roubles, and for priests and various ' cult-servants ' 150 roubles.

Building tax and ground rent

Building tax is paid by private persons, enterprises, institutions, etc. owning dwelling-houses or other buildings. On dwellings belonging to State, co-operative and social enterprises, institutions and organizations the annual tax is one-half per cent of the assessed value of the building; for other buildings, including private dwelling-houses, the tax is one per cent of the value of the building.

' Ground rent ' is an annual fee for a site the use of which has been given for building for an unlimited period of time. The amount of the ground rent varies between 4 and 18 kopeks per square metre according to the type of locality.

Building tax and ground rent are not paid by collective farmers, individual peasants and other persons who pay agricultural tax. There are special regulations granting exemption or reliefs to, among others, members of the armed forces, pensioners and members of the academy of sciences.

Tax on cattle and means of transport

In towns, workers' communities, villa communities and health resorts special dues are levied for the possession of means of transport and cattle (bovines, camels, asses, mules and reindeer).

The dues are lowest in the workers' communities (industrial dense areas) and highest in certain large cities. Thus, for example, the duty for cars and motor-boats varies between 10 and 25 roubles and for motor-cycles between 5 and 15 roubles per horse-power, and for bicycles between 5 and 15 roubles.

Fees at kolkhoz markets

At kolkhoz markets (see p. 101) a special fee is taken from collective farmers and peasants, etc. who sell the products of their own private cultivation, as also from artisans selling their own products or carrying out their craft within the market area, and from private persons who sell their own belongings. The fee is paid for each day, and its size depends on the method of selling: when selling from a table, basket or handcart, the fee is 1 to 3 roubles, when selling from a lorry it is 15 roubles.

Stamp duties

State stamp duties are paid on a large number of occasions by enterprises, private persons, etc. who have recourse to the courts or certain other authorities over matters of a legal or other nature. For example, the notarial authorities charge a special fee for the attestation of a person's right to inherit. This amounts to:

Value of property	Duty
Up to 300 roubles	10 roubles
300 to 1,000 roubles	20 ,,
1,000 ,, 3,000 ,,	50 ,,
3,000 ,, 5,000 ,,	100 ,,
5,000 ,, 10,000 ,,	5 per cent of value
Over 10,000 ,,	10 ,, ,, ,, ,,

Insurance amounts from contracted personal insurance, the value of State bonds, deposits in savings banks and other credit institutions, the value of author's rights and author's fees are not included in the value of the property. If the property consists of nothing but such items, the stamp duty is 10 roubles.

A stamp duty of 15 roubles is paid for registering a marriage. For an application for divorce the duty is usually 100 roubles. If the court grants the divorce there is a stamp duty of 500 to 2,000 roubles to be paid by either one or both parties. Divorce from a spouse condemned to long-term imprisonment or who has vanished or is insane, is registered without duty; in such cases the duty for applying for divorce is 3 roubles.

State loans

A regular feature of the Soviet Union's budget is the State bonds. In certain cases bonds have been issued with fixed rate of interest. Latterly, the most usual form has been that of the lottery-loan. The bonds have been acquired partly by private individuals, partly by certain institutions and organizations such as savings banks, insurance establishments, collective farms and artisan *artels*. Propaganda campaigns on behalf of the State loans have been organized in the press and at places of work and elsewhere. Judging by the Soviet sources available, the wage-earners have bought bonds to an average annual value of several weeks' income, and for them they have been able to pay by successive deductions from their wages, usually spread over ten months. The following particulars should provide a rough idea of the size and extent of this expenditure.

According to Plotnikov's *The Budget of the Socialist State*, before the Second World War the majority of workers and employees were accustomed to acquire bonds every year to a value of two or three weeks' income, and the highest paid to the value of a month's wages. During the war, he says, workers and employees usually subscribed for bonds to the value of a month's wages or more.

In May 1949 the Council of Ministers issued an edict on ' the fourth State loan for the reconstruction and development of the industry and commerce of the Soviet Union '. The loan was to run from 1st October 1949 to 1st October 1969. During this period, for every series of 100 million roubles prizes were to be drawn to a total amount of 89 million roubles; the bonds which drew no prize were to be repaid after the draw at their face value.

The Presidium of the Union's Central Council exhorted 'all those who worked in the Soviet Union' to subscribe to the extent of three or four weeks' income. The Moscow press reported that at various places of work bonds were subscribed by all or nearly all wage-earners; in several such reports names were given of people who had subscribed for a month's wage. The amount of the loan was fixed initially at 20 milliard roubles; according to the budget report 23·6 milliards were received. A corresponding loan in 1950 brought in about 27 milliard roubles.

A textbook published in 1945, *Incomes in the Budget of the Soviet Union*, gives an account of the methods used in planning the issue of loans. Here it is stated, amongst other things: ' Of especial significance in planning the amount of the loan is the extent of the wage fund for workers and employees and the income of collective farmers, as also the balance of the people's monetary income and expenditure. On the basis of what has become the established practice, that the amount subscribed corresponds to 3 weeks' to one month's income from work and that all workers and employees subscribe, it is easy to fix the sum to be aimed at for the urban population, if the amounts subscribed during previous years are also taken into consideration.'

In the years prior to the Second World War the State savings banks were allowed to grant loans for up to six months against the security of State bonds, the amount of the loan being restricted to 30 per cent of the nominal value of the bonds. After the outbreak of war in 1941 the savings banks stopped granting such loans.

It may be mentioned here that State bonds falling due at the time of the monetary reform in December 1947 (*cf.* p. 142) were converted at the reduced values. As a result, certain bonds of older issues were exchanged for bonds in the ' State 3 per cent internal lottery loan ', which was described as 'freely circulating'; according to advertisements in the Soviet press these bonds could be freely bought and sold in the savings banks.

The budget for 1951 allowed for an income of 33·4 milliard roubles from State borrowing from the people and ' State organizations '; the people were to receive prizes from bonds totalling 5 milliard roubles for that year 1951.

CHAPTER X

SOCIAL BENEFITS

THIS chapter deals with those social benefits which are financed in whole or in part out of the public budget. It is concerned mainly with the social insurance for workers and employees, most other forms of social assistance being treated summarily.

State expenditure for social and cultural purposes

In the budget for 1949 the expenditure on social and cultural purposes was estimated at 119,214 million roubles distributed among the following main items as follows:

	Million roubles
Education	60,779
Public Health	21,604
Physical culture	274
Social care (*sotsialnoye obespechenie*)	21,429
State assistance to those with large families and to lone mothers	3,358
State social insurance	11,770

In the statistical report on the implementation of the economic plan for the year 1949, it is stated that during that year the people received 'payments and benefits' of a social or cultural nature to an amount of more than 110 milliard roubles. Special mention is made of assistance and payments through social insurance for workers and employees, pensions through social care, free visits and visits at beneficial rates to sanatoria, rest-homes and children's institutions, assistance to those with large families and to lone mothers, free care of the sick, free education and occupational training, stipendia for students and paid holidays.

According to the report of the Minister of Finance, Zverev, the actual expenditure during 1949 for social and cultural purposes amounted to 116 milliard roubles. The corresponding amounts in the budgets for 1950 and 1951 were 120·7 and 120·8 milliard roubles respectively.

These figures call for a certain amplification.

With regard to education, we have already given particulars of the various types of educational establishments in Chapter III. The following are a few details of the regulations governing the financing of the costs of study.

Fees at certain educational establishments

Education in the first seven classes of the general schools is free. Fees are taken in general schools starting from the eighth class and also at trade middle schools and colleges. An edict of 2nd October 1940 fixed the fees for classes 8 to 10 of middle schools and for the trade middle schools at 200 roubles a year in Moscow, Leningrad and the capitals of the republics of the Union, and to 150 roubles elsewhere. At the same time, the fees for colleges were fixed at 400 roubles a year in Moscow, Leningrad and the capitals of the republics and 300 roubles elsewhere; for art-, dramatic- and music-colleges the fee was 500 roubles. Fees are reduced by half for those taking correspondence courses or attending evening classes and middle schools for adults.

Exemption from paying fees is granted to certain categories of pupils at middle schools and colleges, for example to the children of disabled pensioners, children from children's homes, children of those who fought in the war, of disabled persons, children being maintained by private soldiers or NCOs and the children of officers who fell in the war or were disabled in the war.

Stipendia

Under certain conditions mentioned below, stipendia are paid to pupils at trade middle schools and colleges. According to an edict of 15th September 1943, at certain colleges which trained personnel for industry and transport these stipendia were to be for 210, 240, 275, 275 and 315 roubles a month respectively for each of the five yearly courses. At other colleges the corresponding amounts were 140, 160, 185, 185 and 210 roubles. At certain technical middle schools the stipendia for the first to fourth years' courses were 125, 150, 175 and 200 roubles respectively and at other trade middle schools 80, 100, 120 and 140 roubles a month. For pupils with especially good results the stipendia were to be raised by 25 per cent. Post-graduates (*aspirants*) at the higher educational establishments received 600 or 700 roubles, and aspirants (for a degree) at scientific academies 900 roubles a month. In connection with the increase in the prices of rationed goods made in September 1946 (*cf.* p. 54) the stipendia for those at colleges were raised by 80 roubles a month and for those at trade middle schools by 60 roubles.

The conditions for receiving a stipendium were changed in 1949 in certain respects about which no details are available. A handbook for medical personnel published in 1950 gave the details of the amounts of the stipendia quoted above. It further gave the text of an edict issued by the Ministry of Health in August 1948, according to which, starting from the academic year 1948 to 1949, students taking their first year's course at medical colleges and middle schools should only receive a stipendium if they had obtained excellent or good marks at the entrance examination. According to an advertisement in *Trud* in June 1949 the stipendia at the mining college in Sverdlovsk were 395 roubles a month for the first year and 580 for the last year.

Besides the stipendia mentioned here there are special stipendia for particularly outstanding students, for example the Stalin stipendia.

Care of the sick

On the subject of the *care of the sick*, let me first quote an extract from *The Administrative Law of the Soviet Union*:

' Free medical attention for all workers is the most distinctive feature in the Soviet organization of the care of the people's health. As an exception, fee-charging clinics and nursing institutions and private physician's practice are permitted for persons who wish to avail themselves of treatment for which fees are charged. These activities are none the less carried on under the control of the health authorities.'

The majority of the institutions for general and private nursing are administered by the State health authorities. Certain institutions do come under other organs, for example 'sanatoria' (*cf.* p. 122). According to one reference book on the medical services in Moscow (published in 1947), the people had access to free medical attention (including dentistry) at hospitals and other specialized institutions as well as at the policlinics, etc., serving the population of certain districts or the personnel at certain places of work. At certain policlinics and 'ambulatoria' the public could receive attention against payment; the doctors at fee-taking clinics, like those in private practice, did not have the right to send patients direct to hospitals.

It has not been possible to obtain more detailed information about the quantitative importance of the various forms of medical attention. Maurice Lovell in his *The Soviet Way of Life* (1948) states that it was officially estimated that in 1938 the State paid for more than 90 per cent of the cost of all medical attention given.

According to the Five-year Plan for 1946–1950, the number of beds in hospitals was to be 985,000 in 1950 instead of 710,000 which it had been in 1940. (According to *The Great Soviet Encyclopædia* the figure in the plan only refers to the system of the Ministry of Health.) According to the statistical report of the Central Administration the number of beds in hospitals in 1950 was 25 per cent greater than in 1940. The same source gives the number of doctors in the entire country as having increased by 75 per cent between 1940 and 1950. (*The Great Soviet Encyclopædia* gives the number of doctors in the Soviet Union in 1941 as 130,400.)

Assistance during disablement, in old age and sickness

The State budget provides the means of assisting certain categories of persons who have difficulty in maintaining themselves by reason of disablement, old age or illness, etc. Thus the State social insurance gives assistance, pensions, etc. to workers and employees. Certain forms of assistance are administered by the social care authorities (see below). Members of artisans'- and disabled-persons' co-operatives as well as collective farmers can through the co-operative insurance organizations and mutual-aid funds receive support or loans in the event of sickness, disablement, old age, etc.; such activities fall outside the scope of this book. There are special organizations dealing with the assistance of writers, composers, artists and architects.

Social Care

The authorities administering social care are under the control of the ministries in the various republics of the Union. In *The Soviet Union's Administrative Law* (published in 1950) the main duties of the social care authorities are given as being (1) the sanctioning and payment of pensions; (2) the provision of work for disabled persons partially capable of working; (3) to take care of the aged and other necessitous persons in special institutions (homes for the disabled, for the aged, etc.); (4) the management of certain social organizations (the collective-farm funds for mutual aid, funds for mutual insurance and mutual help in artisan co-operatives, etc.).

The social care authorities administer part of the funds of the social insurance and see to, among other things, the payment of pensions to the disabled and aged, who have ceased to earn wages (see below). This circumstance should explain the difference between the item 'social insurance funds' on the income side and 'social insurance' on the expenditure side of the budget for the year 1949 (*cf.* pp. 97 and 111).

Social insurance

The social insurance comprises almost all categories of workers and employees. Among the exceptions are those who perform temporary and casual work for private employers, for example typists, sempstresses, washerwomen, etc. (but not domestic servants), and also certain personal groups (*e.g.* members of the militia), who receive pensions, assistance, etc. under other arrangements.

Financing

The social insurance is financed by contributions from employers. Generally the insurance contributions are a certain percentage of the amount paid in wages; in 1947 this percentage varied between 3·7 (the artists' association) and 9·6 (the salt industry workers' union).

Forms of assistance

The social insurance gives assistance to workers and employees who by reason of temporary or permanent loss of the ability to work have wholly or partly lost their earnings, and also in certain other cases. The assistance is given in the form of relief and pensions, free or subsidized residence in rest-homes and 'sanatoria' (*cf.* p. 122), subsidies for diet foods, etc., etc. The social insurance is also used to finance certain assistance measures for children, such as camps, 'sanatoria' and such-like.

The total budgetary expenditure on social insurance amounted in 1949 to about 17·5 milliard roubles, which was thus divided:

	Milliard roubles
Benefit during sickness, etc.	4·840
Pensions, etc.	7·228
Benefit during pregnancy and at childbirth ..	1·226
Measures for children (pioneer camps, children's sanatoria, etc.)	·936
Rest-homes and 'sanatoria', tourist organization, dietary foods	1·950
Cultural activities, etc.	·883
Building-work for cultural and similar purposes	·266
Inspection, control of doctors and expenditure on organisation	·162

Administration

The social insurance is administered by the trade union organizations under the control of the All-Union Council, partly in co-operation with the social care authorities.

Within each trade union, the social insurance work of the

local and regional organizations is directed and controlled by the union's central committee, which has, among other things, to check that the insurance contributions are being paid, to work out the union's social insurance budget and report on it to the All-Union Council. The current administration and control of social insurance at places of work are performed by the factory-, workshop- or house-committee with the assistance of a special delegate; thus ' an insurance delegate ' must be elected in each ' union group '; and in larger concerns with separate departmental union committees, departmental commissions for social insurance; and in enterprises with at least a hundred employees, a social insurance council.

Concerns and institutions that employ labour must in their character of ' insurance holder ' be registered with the trade organizations. Concerns must, as has been mentioned, pay an insurance contribution of a certain percentage of the sum paid out in wages. They must assist the trade organizations in their control of the various insurance benefits.

Differentiation of benefits

Social insurance benefits are differentiated with regard to such circumstances as the wage-income of the insured person, the length of his employment with the one concern, the nature of his work, his membership of trade union, etc., etc. In what follows will be found the main rules for the various forms of assistance and certain special regulations for special groups.

Pensions

The social insurance is the means of financing old-age and disablement pensions for workers and officials, pensions for their families after their death and in certain cases pensions for long service. Certain other pensions, for example ' academic pensions ' for scientists and their families as well as ' personal pensions ' for exceptional services, are financed by means of grants made to the social care authorities. These authorities also have to fix the amount of the pensions which are financed with social insurance funds and to see to the payment of the pensions to those pensioners who do not have paid employment.

Entitlement to a pension

As will be explained in more detail later, a certain qualifying period is normally required before a person becomes entitled to a pension. In calculating this qualifying period all, or (in certain cases) a part, of the time the person concerned has had paid employment as a worker or employee is included. In certain cases even military service, partisan activities, time spent on study at certain educational establishments, work as member of a co-operative artisan organization, etc. are counted. Excluded from the qualifying period is any time the person concerned has been under sentence of corrective labour, even though that labour was performed at his normal place of work.

Pensions can be withdrawn or reduced in certain circumstances, for example when a person is taken into a home for the disabled or a lunatic asylum. Pensions are not paid to persons serving a term of imprisonment or who have been ordered into banishment (*ssylka*) or forbidden residence (*vysylka*) (see p. 174). Certain crimes can be punished with loss of entitlement to a pension (see p. 174).

A person who has more than one reason for claiming a pension (for example old age pension and disablement pension, or a long-service pension and personal pension) can himself choose which of the two he shall receive.

Occupational categories

Wage-earners are divided into three categories according to which the size of the pension varies. The *first* category comprises workers and functionaries engaged on work underground and in certain work that is injurious to health; to the *second* category belong workers and functionaries in the ' leading ' industries: metallurgy, engineering, electro-technical industry, coal industry, iron ore, oil, chemical and rubber industries, railways and shipping, concerns producing for communications; and to the *third* category all other workers and functionaries.

Calculation of the amount of pensions

Pensions are calculated according to the regulations for the first or second category, if the pensioner's last employment came into either the first or second category and provided that at least half of the requisite qualifying period can be shown to have been spent in the first or second category (this last condition does not apply however, in the event of accident or occupational disease).

The amount of the pension consists of a certain percentage of the pensioner's average wage-income per month, but the income is usually restricted to a maximum of 300 roubles. In certain cases the regulations are more favourable (see pp. 115–116 and 119).

In conjunction with the increase in the prices of rationed goods in September 1946 a 'dear-times' increment of 60 roubles a month, similar to that added to wages and stipendia, was granted to pensioners who were not earning a wage. Since rationing was abolished, it has been ordered in an edict dated 14th September 1948 that when new pensions are being fixed these additions shall only be paid to those pensioners who are resident in towns and workers' communities. It should be remembered that this 'dear-times' addition is not added to those pensions which are paid on the basis of the following awards.

Old-age pensions

Male workers and functionaries are normally entitled to an old-age pension on their 60th birthday if they have a qualifying period of 25 years of paid work (cf. p. 113). Female workers and officials become entitled to a pension at the age of 55 and for them the qualifying period is 20 years. As a rule all paid employment is counted towards the qualifying period, even though a longish period of time may have elapsed between the different periods of employment. Persons engaged in working underground or in noxious work are entitled to an old-age pension at the age of 50, if they have a qualifying period of 20 years, 10 of which must have been spent in underground or noxious work.

Old-age pensions are authorized irrespective of the state of health of the wage-earner in question and no matter whether he stops working or remains in his employment. Anyone who has ceased to work as worker or employee before reaching pensionable age is not entitled to an old-age pension; should he again take paid employment he will be entitled to an old-age pension, provided he has a sufficiently long qualifying period. Persons who continue working after they have been granted an old-age pension receive the full pension no matter what the size of the income they have from their work.

For wage-earners in the first, second and third occupational categories the old-age pensions amount to 65, 60 and 50 per cent respectively of their wage-income for the previous twelve months. If this wage, however, exceeds 300 roubles a month, the pension will generally be calculated as though it had been 300 roubles a month; for certain categories of wage-earners, for example those in the coal industry, metal industry and chemical industry, there is no maximum for calculating their pension, which is 50 per cent of the basic wage.

Disablement pensions

Disablement pensions are paid to workers and functionaries who have wholly or partly lost their ability to work for a considerable period of time. There is usually the condition that the disabled person should have had paid work for a certain number of years. No such qualifying period is required, however, of persons under the age of 20 or of those who have been disabled through an occupational disease or accident while at work. Otherwise the following qualifying periods are required for persons of different ages:

Age	Years spent in work underground or injurious to health	Years spent in other work:	
		Men	Women
20–22	2	3	2
22–25	3	4	3
25–30	4	6	4
30–35	5	8	5
35–40	6	10	7
40–45	7	12	9
45–50	8	14	11
50–55	10	16	13
55–60	12	18	14
60	14	20	15

The qualifying period does not have to be unbroken, but if more than 5 years have elapsed between two periods of employment, the period prior to that break is not counted in the qualifying period.

The size of the disablement pension depends on the degree of disablement, the causes of it and the occupational category (*cf*. p. 113) to which the wage-earner belonged.

As regards degree of disablement, pensioners are divided into three groups. To the *first group* belong those who have entirely lost their ability to work and require the help of others (for example, the blind). The *second group* comprises those who have entirely lost the ability to work, but do not require help. The *third group* consists of those who are not capable of regular work at their former occupation under normal conditions, but who can use the remains of their ability for irregular work or in another less skilled occupation. The degree of disablement is fixed by special expert medical commissions.

Where disablement is the result of an accident at work or of occupational disease, the pension for those in the first, second and third groups is respectively 100, 75 and 50 per cent of their wage-earnings. Certain injuries received in military service rank equally with accidents at work.

Similarly to the old-age pensions, the disablement pensions are usually calculated on a wage-income not exceeding 300 roubles a month. For certain categories this maximum has been increased to 500 or 600 roubles, besides which the pension can be increased by 10 to 20 per cent of the amount between that maximum and a still higher limit (1,200 or 1,500 roubles).

When disablement has been caused by illness other than an occupational disease or by an accident unconnected with the person's employment, a disablement pension is paid to those who can fulfil the requirement of a certain total number of years' work, as set out in the table on p. 115. For those in the first group, the pension is then 67 to 69 per cent of the wage (depending on their occupational category), for the second group 47 to 49 per cent, and 33 to 35 per cent for those in the third group. Besides this, the disabled in the first and second groups receive a certain percentage added to their pension if they have worked for any considerable length of time in one and the same concern. The actual amounts of these extra percentages are given in the following table:

Trade category	Number of years of uninterrupted employment	Addition per cent of pension
1	3–5	10
	5–10	20
	above 10	25
2	4 – 8	10
	8–12	15
	above 12	20
3	5–10	10
	10–15	15
	above 15	20

If a disabled person in the third group who has not yet reached pensionable age is earning a wage and the total of his wage-income and pension together exceeds the former wage-income which he had before his pension was granted, then his pension is reduced by the amount of the excess, though not by more than 50 per cent of the pension originally sanctioned. Pensions for this category of disabled persons are reduced by 50 per cent if the pensioner resides in the country and is associated with agriculture. On the other hand, the full pension is paid irrespective of possible wage-income to disabled persons in the first and second groups, as also to those in the third group who have reached pensionable age.

Pensions to families of deceased persons

If a worker, employee or person in receipt of a pension from the social insurance dies or is declared 'absent without news', his pension can be paid to the following categories of members of his family who were maintained by that person; (a) children and brothers and sisters under the age of 16 (or, if studying, under the age of 18); (b) grown children and brothers and sisters who became disabled before reaching the age of 16 (if students before the age of 18); (c) parents and spouse, in so far as they are disabled or aged (that is for men over 60 and for women

117

over 55); (d) one of the parents or the spouse, irrespective of ability to work and age, if that person is engaged in caring for the children or brothers and sisters of the deceased person, they being under 8 years of age.

For children maintained by both parents a pension is paid when one parent dies, even if the other continues to work. Other members of families who are provided for by several persons receive assistance (pension) only if the person who dies is the one who contributed most to the maintenance of the member in question.

If the provider died as the result of an accident at work or of an occupational disease or had been in receipt of a pension, the surviving members of his family are entitled to a pension irrespective of the length of time in which he was in paid employment. In other cases the same qualifying period is required as for the granting of a disablement pension.

In fixing the pension to be given to the surviving dependants of a deceased person, the basis is that amount which the deceased himself would have received as his pension had he been a disabled person in the first group. For one dependant without any provision the pension paid would be 50 per cent of the pension thus reckoned, for two dependants 75 per cent, for three dependants 100 per cent, and for four or more dependants 125 per cent.

The pensions for families of deceased persons are paid in full, even if the survivors are earning wages.

Funeral assistance

Funeral assistance is afforded by the social insurance for workers, functionaries, pensioners, students who have previously been workers or functionaries and for their families. The assistance varies between 500 and 200 roubles according to the age of the deceased and the location of the burial (town or country); it does not depend on the length of time the deceased was in paid employment.

Pensions for long service

Pensions for long service are paid out of social insurance funds to certain groups of office-holders with a total of 25 years' service in certain occupations, such as teachers and other functionaries in the educational system, medical and veterinary officers in the country and in workers' communities, as also to agronomists in the country. Teachers and certain other employees in the educational system receive a pension of 40 per cent of their basic salary, there being no maximum. Other groups receive 50 per cent of the average monthly income, though not more than 150 roubles a month. These pensions are paid without reduction, even if the person concerned continues to work.

Assistance in sickness, etc.

Assistance during temporary loss of ability to work ('sick benefit') can be paid out of social insurance funds on certain conditions to (1) persons who by reason of illness are not able to work; (2) persons who by reason of illness have been transferred temporarily to other work for which the pay is lower than their usual employment; (3) persons who by reason of their state of health require care in 'sanatoria' or health resorts (in so far as their holidays do not suffice for this); (4) persons who are nursing an invalid in their family; (5) people who because of the danger of infection are kept in quarantine or forbidden by the health authorities to carry out their normal work (for example, in the foodstuffs industry).

This assistance is intended to make up for lost earnings either entirely or in part. Workers and employees can also receive assistance from the social insurance for certain special forms of care, for example in 'sanatoria', rest-homes and health resorts, as well as for additional dietary foods.

As a general rule workers and employees are entitled to sickness benefit from the day they take up a position, if they lose the ability to work during the time they are in paid employment (including any trial period), and the assistance is paid throughout the duration of the illness or until the wage-earner has been declared disabled and transferred to a disablement pension. There are, however, special regulations for certain categories.

Disabled persons who work, that is to say persons in receipt of a disablement pension who nevertheless have paid employment, are entitled to sickness benefit for not more than 2 consecutive months and at the most 3 months altogether in any one calendar year.

Seasonal workers and employees receive sickness benefit provided that they have been in paid employment for at least three months during the year preceding the inception of their illness (inability to work) or for at least ten months during the previous two years. If, however, their inability to work has been caused by an accident during work or by occupational disease, sickness benefit will be paid irrespective of the length of time the person concerned has been at work. If the incapacity was due to other causes, the rule generally in force is that sickness benefit will be paid for 75 days at the most; thereafter, if the union primary organization so decides, further assistance may be paid but to a limited extent.

Workers and officials who have been dismissed for infringement of labour discipline, or crime, or who voluntarily left their previous place of work, are not entitled to sickness benefit until they have worked at least 6 months at their new place of work.

The Labour Laws of the Soviet Union states that it has become the accepted practice that this rule of a six-months interval is not applied when a wage-earner has changed his job and his previous employer was obliged to agree to his going (see p. 40).

Excluded from the right to sickness benefit are malingerers, those who have deliberately contracted a disease, who have not complied with the instructions of a doctor or who stay away from medical examination without sufficient reason; persons who have been condemned to corrective labour for truancy (*cf.* p. 88) lose the right to assistance for six months after being sentenced. Those who become ill in consequence of a drinking bout lose their right to sickness benefit for the first five days; from and including the sixth day, only half the benefit is paid if the person concerned is without the obligation to support child, spouse or parents.

This sickness benefit amounts to a certain proportion (at the most 100 per cent) of the wage-income. For workers and officials who belong to a trade union benefit is paid, with certain exceptions, according to the following table and depends on the time the person concerned has been employed without break at the same concern or institution:

Period of Employment	Assistance, per cent of wage
Above 8 years	100
5–8 „	80
3–5 „	60
under 3 „	50

For persons in trade unions and under the age of 18 the sickness benefit paid is 60 per cent of the wage, irrespective of the period of employment. Persons who do not belong to a trade union receive half the amount paid to those in trade unions.

For certain categories the regulations are more favourable. Thus, certain groups of trade union workers and employees in the coal-, metal- and chemical industries receive assistance amounting to 100 per cent of their wages after one year's employment or if they are victims of an accident while working or are stricken by an occupational disease, and to 60 per cent if their employment has lasted less than a year.

War-disabled persons working in concerns and institutions receive sickness benefit of 100 per cent of their wages irrespective of the length of their employment.

If a wage-earner is transferred temporarily to other work because of illness, he receives sickness benefit in accordance with the general norms, but the sum of the assistance paid to him and of his wage at the new place of work must not exceed his previous wage-income.

Assistance is calculated on the basis of the actual wage-income (not counting overtime and certain other extras) immediately prior to the onset of the illness. For piece-workers and others who have a basic wage plus additions, bonuses etc., the assistance is reckoned at the most at twice the basic wage. The maximum amount for sickness benefit is 160 roubles a day.

In calculating the period of unbroken employment on which the size of the benefit depends, it is not only the period the person concerned has worked at one place of work that is counted, but any periods of military service or partisan activities are also included. The period of employment is considered to be unbroken if the person concerned has been transferred to another place of work within one and the same ' system ' in accordance with the decision of a superior organ (for example, if a wage-earner is transferred from one railway to another in accordance with a decision of the Ministry of Transport). Further, a break in the period of employment or a change of place of work is not counted in the following, among other cases: (1) If due to absence on certain public business; (2) if due to dismissal as a result of reduction in staff or of cessation of the enterprise, provided the break in employment does not exceed one month; (3) In the event of temporary disablement, if the wage-earner returns to his previous place of work or presents a certificate to say that he cannot be given suitable work at his former place of work; (in this case, however, the period of absence is not counted in with the period of unbroken employment); (4) When the wage-earner changes his (or her) place of work because the wife (or husband) has been transferred to another district, provided the break in employment does not exceed a month over and above the length of the journey; (5) When a pregnant woman or a woman with a child under one year old moves to another place of work in the locality where she resides; (6) When the wage-earner has been studying at an educational establishment in accordance with the decision of a State institution, economic or social organization; included in the period of unbroken employment is time spent at a trade school (for 'labour reserves'), but not time spent in study at other educational establishments.

Finally, it must be mentioned that during the Second World War special regulations were issued concerning the calculation of the qualifying period in connection with evacuation and residence in occupied territory.

Sanatoria and rest-homes

The social insurance organization owns a number of 'sanatoria' and rest-homes, where the workers and employees may stay gratis or for a certain fee (cf. p. 111). A number of similar establishments are run by the State health authorities and by other authorities, concerns and organizations. There are a number of 'night sanatoria' and prophylactories, where workers and employees receive preventative treatment without stopping work;

these establishments are organized by the concerns and financed with social insurance funds.

The Russian expression 'sanatoria' rendered here as 'sanatorium' refers to several different types of establishment for the care of the sick and for convalescence: there are sanatoria for the care of tuberculosis, nervous diseases, diseases of the heart and blood vessels, of the stomach and intestines, for general care and convalescence, for pregnant women and mothers with children. It should be emphasized that the health authorities also maintain special hospitals and other establishments for the treatment of tuberculosis.

Every year the trade organizations issue a certain number of warrants for travel to and residence in sanatoria and rest-homes for workers and employees. One-fifth of the warrants for sanatoria and one-tenth of the warrants for rest-homes have to be issued gratis, while the others involve paying 30 per cent of the cost; the remaining 70 per cent is paid out of social insurance funds. The free warrants are to be issued in the first place to workers who have made great contributions to production, to war-disabled, to young workers, pregnant women and nursing-mothers.

Wage-earners who in accordance with the verdict of a medical 'sanatoria- and health-resort commission' are sent for treatment to a sanatorium can in certain circumstances, in addition to the grant towards the treatment itself, receive sickness benefit through the social insurance in accordance with the regulations to which we have already referred on p. 119. Here a distinction is made between those fit to work (e.g. rheumatics) and those not fit, that is to say those who are already listed as sick when they are remitted for sanatorium treatment (for example, people with acute tuberculosis).

Persons capable of working receive leave with sickness benefit, if they have been directed through a trade union organization (gratis or paying 30 per cent), but not if they have been directed through other channels (e.g. through the concern's management) or are themselves paying for their stay. They must first use up their holidays; for example, if 34 days are spent in travelling to and from the sanatorium and in having treatment, and the wage-earner has 14 days' holiday, he is paid sickness benefit for the remaining 20 days.

The not-fit-to-work receive sickness benefit no matter who pays for their treatment, and the benefit is paid for the whole duration of the treatment, in this case with a deduction for the period by which the holidays exceed one month. According to Kuznetsov's report (*cf.* Chapter II), in 1948 the trade union organizations remitted about 2 million workers and employees to sanatoria and rest-homes.

Diet foods

Workers and employees can receive from the social insurance a contribution towards the cost of *diet foods*; this subsidy is paid direct to the eating-place which supplies the food. The employees themselves pay part of the cost. Thus persons with families pay for diet food 40 per cent of that part of the family's total wage-income which on the average would fall to the lot of one member of the family, and persons without dependants pay 25 per cent of their wage-income. In either case, however, there is a maximum payment of 250 roubles a month.

Social insurance benefit during pregnancy and childbed

Female workers and employees are entitled during pregnancy and childbirth to 77 days' leave, of which 35 are taken prior to confinement and 42 afterwards. With abnormal births or when more than one child is born the period of leave after confinement is prolonged to 56 days. If the period of leave prior to confinement turns out to be longer or shorter than 35 days (for example because the doctor estimated the date wrongly), the period of leave after confinement remains the same, 42 (or 56) days. Women who have had uninterrupted employment with the same concern or institution for at least three months receive assistance through the social insurance throughout the period of their leave. As with sickness benefit, this assistance is a certain percentage of the woman's wage-income. This percentage is graduated according to the woman's total period of paid employment and the length of time she has worked at a stretch for one and the same concern. This assistance in pregnancy and childbirth amounts to 100 per cent of the woman's wage-income during the whole period of her leave if the woman is a member of a trade union and has also had paid employment for at least 3 years and has been employed in the same concern or institution for two years without a break. The assistance is similarly 100 per cent of the wage-income for female Stakhanovites and 'shock-workers'—that is to say, the élite of women workers—who have been in paid employment for at least a year, for women under the age of 18 who have worked for at least a year at one place of work, and to women disabled in war, to partisans and those decorated with the orders of the Soviet Union and its republics.

Women employed for at least 2 years in the same concern but who have not had paid employment for a total of at least 3 years, and also women under 18 who have not been employed by the same concern for a whole year, are paid assistance amounting to 75 per cent of their wage-income during the first 20 days of their leave and to 100 per cent thereafter. Women with 1 to 2 years' unbroken employment in one concern receive in assistance two-thirds of their wage-income during 20 days and thereafter 100 per cent, while women under the age of 18 with less than one year's employment are paid two-thirds of their wage-income during the whole period of leave.

The rules about the period of employment are more favourable for certain trade groups, among them the coal and building industries and the railways.

Female workers and employees who are not members of a trade union receive in assistance 50 per cent of their wage during the first 30 days of their leave and thereafter two-thirds. Those disabled in war, however, receive 100 per cent of their wages, even though they are not members of a union.

Besides the benefits mentioned here, social insurance funds can be used to give assistance for newborn children, intended for the purchase of food and clothes. The whole benefit amounts to 300 roubles, 220 of which are paid when the child is born and 80 when it is five months old. It is paid if the child's mother or father have worked for the same concern without a break for at least three months and if the parent applying for assistance has had an income not exceeding 500 roubles during the last few months.

Assistance for lone mothers and those with large families

An edict of 27 June 1936 introduced State assistance of a single payment of 2,000 roubles for every child after the sixth. On 8th July 1944 a ukase was promulgated ' concerning the extension of State assistance to pregnant women, unmarried mothers and those with many children, enhanced protection for mothers and children, the introduction of the title "Heroine Mother" and the foundation of the order "Motherhood's Glory" and the "motherhood medal"'. This ukase contained regulations extending the period of leave for pregnancy and increasing the social insurance benefits for pregnant women, made certain alterations in the legislation concerning divorce and the taxation of lone persons, and increased the State subsidy for mothers with large families and special assistance for unmarried mothers. The amount of this State child subsidy was reduced shortly before the monetary reform of 1947 (*cf.* p. 142).

This child subsidy is paid to married women and widows with three or more children, and in part to lone mothers whatever the number of their children. In contrast to the benefits from social insurance with which we have so far dealt, this is paid irrespective of the woman's social position (even to women who are not workers or employees).

Married women and widows receive either an outright payment or a monthly sum while the child is between the ages of 2 and 5. The amounts paid are as follows (in roubles):

						Outright payment	Monthly subsidy
On birth of			3rd child	..	..	200	—
,,	,,	,,	4th child	..	..	650	40
,,	,,	,,	5th ,,	..	..	850	60
,,	,,	,,	6th ,,	..	..	1,000	70
,,	,,	,,	7th ,,	..	..	1,250	100
,,	,,	,,	8th ,,	..	..	1,250	100
,,	,,	,,	9th ,,	..	..	1,750	125
,,	,,	,,	10th ,,	..	..	1,750	125
,,	,,	,,	each subsequent child			2,500	150

In fixing the subsidy it is not just the mother's own children which are counted, but also her adoptive children and her husband's children by a previous marriage, in so far as they came under the mother's care before reaching the age of 12; children

who have died are not counted unless they were killed or dis-
appeared during the Second World War, nor are children who
are foreign subjects. If a mother who is entitled to a subsidy dies,
the subsidy can be paid to the children's father or guardian, if
he has to care for some of the deceased mother's children.

Unmarried mothers with one, two and three or more children
born in 1944 or later receive a subsidy of 50, 75 and 100 roubles
a month respectively until the children reach the age of 12; apart
from that, they are entitled to the same subsidies as married
women with children. The additional benefit paid to lone mothers
does not apply if the children are kept in a children's home or
if the mother receives a maintenance allowance for them. For
children born after 8th July 1944, a mother has not the right to
require maintenance allowance of the father if she has not been
married to him.

Institutions caring for children

The social insurance and other general funds contribute to the
establishment and maintenance of various institutions which care
for children, such as crèches, kindergartens, pioneer camps etc.

In towns and industrial localities the health authorities organize crèches which look after children from the age of 4 weeks to
3 years. According to an announcement from the Ministry of
Health the task of the crèches is ' to give working mothers who
have children of crèche age the opportunity of taking part in the
economic, cultural, social and political life of the country and to
help the mothers to rear healthy, spirited children '. The crèches
have to create suitable conditions for the children's development
and upbringing, counteract infirmity among the children and
help in improving the care and upbringing of the children by
raising the standard of hygiene and culture in their homes.

Crèches in towns and industrial localities have to take in children
whose mothers work in concerns or institutions or who are studying. The children are accepted on the direction of the local health
authorities or of the trade union organization at the place of work
which the crèche serves, once the conditions in the child's home
have been investigated and the child itself medically examined.

Kindergartens, playing-grounds and such institutions for children between the ages of 3 and 7 are organized by the authorities

for popular education or by enterprises, institutions, collective farms or co-operative organizations. Their teaching activities are controlled by the authorities for popular education.

Sites for kindergartens have to be distributed by the authorities for popular education or by the management of the concern in question in conjunction with its union organizations, and these latter also have to co-operate in controlling the activities of the kindergartens. Children of union members have priority for kindergartens and crèches.

As a rule children remain in kindergartens not more than 9 hours a day. In exceptional cases, however, the children of lone mothers may stay longer, if necessary the whole 24 hours. The children are given food three times a day if they remain in the kindergarten for 10 hours, and four times if they remain for 12 hours or the entire day and night.

The activities of crèches and kindergartens are financed in part by fees paid by parents (or those persons who have care of the children). The fees differ according to the incomes of the families (from wages, pensions, stipendia, maintenance allowance and State child subsidy). According to the regulations issued in 1948 the fees to be paid are as set out in the following table (in roubles per month):

Income per month (roubles):	Up to 400	401 to 600	601 to 800	801 to 1,200	Over 1,200
Kindergartens in towns and workers' communities:					
9–10 hours per day	40	55	70	85	100
12–14 ,, ,, ,,	50	69	88	106	125
24 ,, ,, ,,	60	83	105	128	150
' Sanatorium-kindergarten ' and stay in country	80	110	140	170	200
Kindergarten in country:					
9–10 hours per day	30	45	60	75	90
12–14 ,, ,, ,,	38	56	75	94	113
24 ,, ,, ,,	45	68	90	113	135
' Sanatorium-kindergarten ' and stay in country	60	90	120	150	180

Income per month (*roubles*):	Up to 400	401 to 600	601 to 800	801 to 1,200	Over 1,200
Crèches in towns and workers' communities:					
9–10 hours per day ..	30	40	50	65	80
12–14 ,, ,, ,, ..	38	50	63	81	100
24 ,, ,, ,, ..	45	60	75	98	120
' Sanatorium-crèches ' and stay in country ..	60	80	100	130	160
Crèches in country:					
9–10 hours per day ..	15	25	35	50	65
12–14 ,, ,, ,, ..	19	31	44	63	81
24 ,, ,, ..	23	38	53	75	98
' Sanatorium-crèches ' and stay in country ..	30	50	70	100	130

In certain cases the fees are reduced for families with several children. Thus parents with 3 children and a total income of not more than 400 roubles a month pay half-fees, as do those with 4 children and an income not exceeding 600 roubles, or with 5 or more children, and for these latter there is no maximum income. Unmarried mothers with a monthly income of not more than 600 roubles likewise pay half-fees.

According to the Five-year Plan for 1946–1950 there were to be kindergartens with places for 2,260,000 children in 1950. The number of places in permanent crèches was to reach 1,251,000 in 1950.

Pioneer camps which have the task of organizing summer holidays for children between the ages of 7 and 14 are organized by the authorities and trade unions. They are financed partly through the social insurance, partly with contributions from the trade unions' own budgets, from the ' director's funds ' (see p. 61), and prizes which concerns may have won in the ' socialist competition ' (see p. 62). A number of free places in pioneer camps are issued to the children of fallen soldiers, disabled soldiers and workers, as well as to the children of low-paid workers

I

and employees or of parents with several children. For other placcs the parents pay part of the cost.

According to Kuznetsov's report (see Chapter II), in 1940 over 4 million children stayed in the pioneer camps of the trades unions and the various authorities. The corresponding figure for 1949 was 5 million.

CHAPTER XI

PROVISION OF DWELLINGS AND CHARGES FOR RENT

IN the Soviet Union, dwelling-houses can be erected and managed by public concerns and institutions, by co-operative and social organizations—for example, the consumers' co-operative, dwellings-co-operative and trade union organizations—and also by private persons.

In 1937 the great bulk of the dwellings owned or rented by the dwellings-co-operative associations were transferred to public concerns and authorities. The dwellings market in the towns is nowadays dominated by public tenement houses and private own-home dwellings.

Statistics on the provision of dwellings

The following statistics will throw some light on the development made in the provision of dwellings. It should be pointed out that in the legislation and statistics dealing with housing, it is usual to use the term ' dwelling surface ', meaning floor space in actual living-rooms. Secondary space such as kitchen, bathroom, lavatory, corridors, etc. is not as a rule included in the ' dwelling surface '.

The available statistics on the state of dwellings are not unanimous. B. P. Veselovsky, for example, gives the following estimates of the ' number of dwellings in the towns ' (cf. p. 181). At the beginning of 1928 it was estimated that there were about 163 million square metres of ' dwelling surface ', of which 77 million were in ' socialized ' (State, co-operative, etc.) buildings and 86 million in privately owned dwellings. The figure at the beginning of 1939 was estimated at about 225 million square metres, of which 140 million were in socialized, and 85 million in privately owned dwellings.

In *The Dwelling—and municipal administration of the Soviet*

131

Union, A. A. Zaslavsky gives the following particulars of the destruction and rebuilding of dwellings during and after the war of 1941–1945: ' Of the 2,567,000 dwelling-houses in the occupied towns of the Soviet Union 1,209,000 were destroyed and ruined, that is to say, more than 50 per cent of the dwelling surface in those towns. . . . During the year 1943–1944 there were repaired and built 12,177,000 sq. m. of dwelling space in the towns and workers' communities in the districts so far recovered. . . . At the end of 1945 the State dwelling fund in the towns had almost reached its pre-war level despite the tremendous damage done by the war '.

According to the Five-year Plan, between 1946 and 1950 72·4 million sq. m. of dwelling surface were to be added in the towns and urban communities through new building and reconstruction under public administration and 12 million sq. m. through the building of individual dwellings. The plan further anticipated considerable expenditure on repairing old dwellings. In the country districts the collective farmers and peasants, with the help of State credits, were to build or repair 3·4 million dwelling-houses.

According to the statistical report of the central administration, during 1946–1950 in the towns and urban communities houses were built or repaired having a total dwelling surface of over 100 million sq. m. and in the country 2·7 million dwelling-houses.

Rent legislation

In the legislation applicable to the whole Soviet Union, there are certain regulations concerning the letting and rents of dwellings; in addition, there are special regulations issued by the various republics. The following particulars about this are taken mostly from D. L. Broner's *Course in Dwelling Economics.*

The ' State dwelling stock ' comprises houses managed by the municipal authorities (town soviets, etc.) and the houses of the State enterprises and institutions.

The municipal authorities can let rooms, apartments or smaller houses (with a maximum of 60 sq. m. dwelling surface) to private citizens or lease houses to State enterprises and institutions, social organizations, etc. In the first case, the agreement can be concluded with any adult member of the family whomsoever. In the case of houses which are owned or in the hands of concerns, institutions, etc. the dwellings are usually let out to those who are employed by that concern or institution, and the agreements concluded grant the tenants the right to retain the dwellings only so long as their employment lasts (*cf.* p. 17).

The apartments in the houses built by dwelling-co-operative building associations are let to the associations' members. The owner of a private house can let dwellings by verbal or written agreement.

Agreements

When a concern, municipal organ or such organization concludes an agreement to rent with a private person, the concern, etc. in question (henceforward we shall use the expression 'landlord') must undertake to put at the disposition of the tenant a space suitable for a dwelling, and to keep the dwelling in serviceable order during the period the agreement remains in force. The landlord shall at his own expense and in good time undertake the necessary major repairs to the tenement he is renting and pay for certain current repairs, such as replacement of doors and windows on account of normal wear-and-tear, repair of floors, stoves, fireplaces, central heating, water-pipes, drainage pipes, electric wiring to light points, and gas and bathroom equipment; the landlord further undertakes to make good all faults and damage in the tenement not later than three days after the tenant's reporting it and to compensate the tenant for losses if faults and damage are not made good within that time.

Obligations of the tenant

In the agreement the tenant undertakes to use the tenement for its intended purpose and to take good care of it, to keep it clean and in habitable shape and also when necessary, but not less than once every three years, at his own expense to carry out certain repairs within the tenement, for example whitewashing ceilings, painting or papering walls, painting floors, window-frames and doors and replacement of glass. The tenant must observe the rules of conduct in force and pay his rent at the time appointed.

He does not have the right to transfer his rights and obligations under the agreement to a third party. The tenant's family participate in all the rights and obligations set out in the agreement.

Agreements to rent are concluded for periods of not more than five years. Sitting tenants who have fulfilled their obligations in accordance with the agreement have priority in making a new agreement, when the old expires.

Sub-letting

Parts of a rented tenement can be sublet with the permission of the landlord. Such sub-letting must not be exploited to obtain an income without working. If a tenant sublets a separate room with speculative intent, he may be deprived of the right to use that room.

Under certain conditions tenants may by agreement exchange tenements.

Dwelling norms and surplus

By various edicts ' dwelling norms ' or ' dwelling-sanitary norms' have been fixed for the various republics and individual places. By these terms is meant ' the minimum expanse of useful dwelling surface due to one person from the enjoyment of a dwelling under an agreement to rent ', that is to say, the surface for which his right of use and enjoyment is protected for the period during which the agreement is valid.

In the legislation of the RSFSR 9 sq. metres per person is given as the dwelling-sanitary norm; but regulations have been issued reducing this norm for certain areas devastated by war. In the Ukraine before the war the sanitary dwelling norm was 13·65 sq. metres per person.

The dwelling surface in excess of the sanitary dwelling norm is called the *surplus*. If such a surplus should be created in the form of separate rooms during the period of an agreement to rent, for example because one or more members of the family have moved from the tenement, the landlord may dispose of these rooms as he sees fit. A tenant may not be deprived of a surplus room, however, if this would result in persons of different sexes (apart from husband and wife and children under 10 years of age) having to sleep in one room, or if husband and wife would have to sleep in separate rooms.

Certain categories of person are entitled to extra dwelling surface above the norm; these are heroes of the Soviet Union, heroes of socialist labour, holders of Orders, etc. and also those who require extra space for their occupation; scientists, writers, artists, inventors, etc.; holders of responsible office in State institutions, concerns and social organizations, certain senior officers of the armed forces; persons suffering from certain diseases.

Cancellation of an agreement to rent

If the tenant does not dwell in the tenement he has rented, the agreement to rent becomes void. In certain cases, however, an absentee tenant can retain his right to the dwelling: this is the case, for example, with those who have gone away for not more than six months, with persons who are ill, under arrest, studying or called-up.

A tenant has the right to give notice before expiry without advancing reasons. An agreement can be terminated before expiry at the request of the landlord in the following cases: if the tenant or his family have systematically destroyed or damaged the tenement or common space; if the tenant or his family behave in such a way that it is impossible for other residents to live at the same time in the same dwelling or room; if the tenant, without good reason, neglects to pay his rent within 3 months of its falling due; if the tenant has temporarily moved with his family to another district and has not returned at the time agreed; if speculation in dwelling space (buying and selling of rooms, fictitious exchanges, sub-letting of rooms for a rent obviously in excess of the norm-ed rent) is discovered.

If the tenant dwells in a house which is administered by a concern, an institution or such organization, and his right to his dwelling is bound up with his employment with that concern, he and his family may be compelled to move from the dwelling if he ends his employment. In certain cases there is a requirement that the matter be tried by a court. Legislation makes a distinction between the following cases:

135

(1) If the tenant has terminated his employment with a State *enterprise* (factory, workshop, etc.) in a house owned by which he has been given a dwelling, the landlord (the enterprise) has the *right* to cancel the agreement to rent and order the tenant to move without finding him another dwelling. But if the tenant ended his employment by reason of disability, accident or because he was called-up for military service or because he had been chosen for another office or transferred to other work, the landlord can require him to move only if he can be offered a suitable dwelling in another house. If a person who has been allowed to rent a dwelling in conjunction with his employment dies, his family has the right to retain the dwelling if another is not provided.

(2) If a tenant has terminated his employment at his own request or been dismissed for infringement of discipline or for crime, the landlord is *bound* to order him to move without finding him another dwelling.

(3) If the tenant has been dismissed from a State *institution* (for example, office, school, etc.) or a social organization for reasons not connected with himself, the landlord has the *right* to order the tenant to move, but is then bound to find him another dwelling.

In certain cases a tenant may even be required to move without another dwelling being found for him; this would be the case, for example, with ' unauthorized ' persons living in a house belonging to the armed forces, transport system or Ministry of the Interior, in student homes, staff residences of hospitals, etc.

Regulation of rents

Rents in towns and urban communities are graded according to the size of the tenement, its equipment and quality, and also with regard to the social position, income and family of the tenant.

The rent is generally calculated on the ' dwelling surface ', that is to say the net floor space in actual living-rooms (*cf*. p. 134). If auxiliary rooms, for example a kitchen or storeroom, are merely used as dwellings, then rent is paid for them as for living-rooms.

In each town, the local authorities fix a standard rent (*osnovnaya stavka kvartirnoi plati*) per sq. metre of dwelling space in a normally equipped dwelling. This standard rent must be not less than 30 kopeks and not more than 44 kopeks per sq. metre per month. Where accommodation is above or below the normal there is a 'tenement tariff' fixed, whereby the rent is increased by additions for special comforts (such as gas, a bathroom, hot water) or reduced because of defects (such as long distance from the centre of the town, no piped water, no drainage or no electricity). Further, special reductions are made for defects in particular rooms or individual tenements in a house, for example, for dark, dingy or damp rooms. The ' tenement tariff' which is left after making deductions from, or additions to, the standard rent, may not be less than 5·5 kopeks per sq. metre per month.

With the ' tariff' for a certain tenement fixed the rent actually paid for it may still vary, as this will depend on the social position, income and family circumstances of the tenant and the density of occupation. For every tenant a basic rent is fixed (which is adopted) for that part of the dwelling surface that corresponds to the so-called paying norm. In the RSFSR the minimum for this norm is 9 sq. metres per person.

For workers and officials with a monthly income of at least 145 roubles the basic rent per sq. metre per month is equivalent to the ' tenement tariff' plus 3·3 kopeks for every full 10 roubles by which the tenant's income exceeds 145 roubles. Thus, for example, the additional amount to be paid with an income of from 245 to 254 roubles is 33 kopeks, and with an income of from 415 to 424 roubles 89·1 kopeks per sq. metre per month. In calculating this the basis taken is the earned income of that member of the family who has the highest income. For workers and officials the basic rent thus fixed may not exceed 1.32 roubles per sq. metre per month. If the local authorities so decide, the basic rent may be reduced by from 5 to 15 per cent if the tenant has to provide for four or more persons on an income of under 30 roubles a month.

For that part of the tenement corresponding to the paying-norm—which, as already mentioned, amounts to 9 sq. metres per member of the family, (a domestic servant being reckoned as a member of the family)—the basic rent is paid. Workers and employees pay basic rents for a further 4·5 square metres, calculated on the whole family. Similarly, only basic rent is paid for the surplus dwelling space that falls to certain categories (*cf.* p. 135). For other surplus dwelling space three times the basic rent is paid, or, if the basic rent is lower than the tenement-tariff, three times the latter. The faultiest part of the tenement, where the rent is lowest, is defined as surplus for this calculation.

Besides the basic rent, the tenant has to pay special charges for central heating and municipal services such as water, drainage, collection of refuse, electricity and gas. The expenses of the administrator of the house on central heating are paid by the tenants in proportion to the rents they pay, provided the costs do not exceed 40 per cent of the rent; excess costs are divided between the tenants in proportion to the dwelling space they occupy but irrespective of the rents they pay. The expense of lighting is divided between the tenants in proportion to the capacity of their light points and—in the case of common spaces—the number of residents. Gas is paid for in accordance with actual consumption or—if there is no individual check or agreement among the tenants—with the number of persons in the family. The charges for water and drainage are shared among the tenants with reference to the equipment of the tenements.

Private persons who own or rent a dwelling-house are entitled to sublet dwellings to other persons for a rent not exceeding 20 per cent above the rate they themselves pay.

These facts about the fixing of rents can be supplemented by the following extract from an article by V. Prokofiev, ' Soviet—the land of low rents ' in *News from the Soviet Union* (1949: 57).

' It has previously been said that the size of the rent is calculated according to the income of the tenant. The law here means not the total income of all persons in the family, but only that of the person in the family with the highest income. Let us, for example, imagine a family in which three persons work: the father is a worker, the son an apprentice and the daughter is studying. If the father has 1,500 roubles a month and the son 800, and the daughter has a monthly stipendium of 350 roubles, then the rent that family pays is 1 rouble 32 kopeks per sq. metre, provided they are not entitled to special reductions. Let us assume that this family has a five-roomed tenement of 60 sq. metres actual dwelling space. The rent is then roughly 80 roubles a month, which amounts to something over 5 per cent of the father's income and only 3 per cent of the family's total income.

'For central heating, water and drainage, gas and electricity that family would pay the municipality a fee equivalent to 5·8 per cent of the father's income or 4 per cent of the family's total income. The entire amount paid—for the dwelling and the municipal services—thus amounts to roughly 11 per cent of the father's income or 7 per cent of the total family income.

'A tenant is not obliged to pay any other charges. The agreement to rent only binds him to avoid neglect and to keep the tenement in as good shape as possible and at his own expense repair minor damage to the paint in the rooms. All major repairs, such, for example, as those to stoves, heating-pipes and elements, water and drainage pipes, electrical and gas and bathroom equipment, laying or replacing floors, windows, doors, etc. are the concern of the letting-organization and are paid for out of funds from the rent-incomes.'

Building of own homes

According to a ukase of 26th August 1948 every citizen of the Soviet Union has the right to buy or build for himself with the right of personal ownership a dwelling-house of one or two storeys with 1 to 5 rooms, either in a town or outside a town.

With the approval of the concern employing them, workers and employees may obtain loans for building their own homes from the municipal banks, which grant such loans within the limits of the amounts which the authorities have fixed for the various branches and enterprises. In each enterprise the director, in conjunction with the factory committee, must draw up a list of the workers and employees who can be given loans and of the size of the loans themselves. The loans are issued by the bank through the concern in question. They may not exceed 10,000 roubles for each person building his own home; they bear interest at 2 per cent and have to be repaid in 7 years. Sites are rented by the local authorities. The local authorities, the concern itself and the trade union organizations have to help to organize the supply of material, transport, etc.

Workers and employees who have been granted a building loan are bound to contribute at least 30 per cent of the value of the building either in the form of cash or of their own labour. A person who has obtained a loan may not sell what he has built with the loan without the consent of the bank.

If a worker or official who has obtained a building loan ends his employment at his own request or is dismissed for infringement of discipline or for crime, he may retain ownership of the building only if his own contribution, including the part of the loan he has repaid, exceeds 50 per cent of the worth of the building and if he repays the outstanding balance of the loan within six months. Otherwise, the building is taken over by the concern, which must repay the builder's contribution to him within three months.

Separate regulations have been drawn up concerning the erection under State administration of homes for sale to workers and employees.

CHAPTER XII

THE PRICES OF CONSUMERS' GOODS AND SERVICES

Retailing organization

IN the Soviet Union the sale of consumers' goods is effected to a large extent through State and co-operative trading establishments. Besides these, producers like collective-farmers, peasants, private craftsmen, etc. have the right to sell their products direct to the consumer. To act as middleman professionally is, on the other hand, forbidden (see p. 13).

State retail trade—including the restaurant and café business and others—is organized partly by the Ministry of Trade, partly by certain other ministries selling special products, and finally by the ' departments for the provisioning of workers ' (ORS) which are linked to individual concerns and which, among other things, see to the service of dining-rooms, buffets and such-like at a place of work or in its vicinity.

The consumers' co-operative association that before the war mostly sold in the country has since 1947 also developed an extensive business in the towns and industrial communities. Even the producers'-co-operatives organization—the co-operatives of artisans and disabled persons, etc.—has its own selling establishments.

In the ' kolkhoz trading ' which is done at the markets, in market-halls, etc. both collective farmers and peasants who do not belong to a collective take part.

The products of State industry are sold in State establishments and those of the consumers' co-operatives. The State establishments have for sale the agricultural products which the collective-farms and private peasants are ordered to supply or have sold in fulfilment of special contracts with State purchasing organs ('centralized buying'), as well as the products of the State farms themselves (*sovhozes*). After the collective-farmers have fulfilled their obligations to the State, they may sell the remaining surplus direct to consumers or to the State and co-operative buying organs (' decentralized purchasing ').

Regulation of retail prices

The retail prices of goods from State concerns and of agricultural products which are obtained through ' centralized purchasing ' are regulated by State edict. The consumers' co-operative organizations regulate their prices for goods from their own enterprises and agricultural products obtained by ' decentralized purchase ' in accordance with precise directives. In kolkhoz trading, the prices vary with supply and demand.

During the war rationing was introduced for the majority of the more important consumers' goods and the prices of these rationed goods were kept very much at the pre-war level. At the same time, unrationed goods were sold in the State shops at ' commercial ' prices, which were several times higher than those of the rationed goods; the same was the case with the agricultural products sold in the open market.

In September 1946 an increase in the prices of rationed goods was put into effect in State shops, and simultaneously the ' dear-times bonus ' that we have already mentioned was introduced, for wage-incomes below 900 roubles a month (*cf.* p. 54) and for certain stipendia (*cf.* p. 108) and pensions (*cf.* p. 114).

The 1947 Monetary Reform

On 14th December 1947 an edict was issued for monetary reform and abolishing the rationing of foodstuffs and manufactured goods.

This monetary reform exchanged the notes in circulation for new notes, in the process of doing which their nominal value was reduced to one-tenth. People's deposits in savings banks and in the State bank were reduced, except the first 3,000 roubles, which retained their old value; amounts between 3,000 and 10,000 roubles were reduced by one-third and any amount above 10,000 roubles by one-half. The balances of the co-operative organizations and the collective-farmers were reduced by one-fifth.

State bonds in circulation were converted in conjunction with the monetary reform, except for the ' second State loan for the reconstruction and development of the industrial and commercial life of the Soviet Union ' issued in 1947. Bonds of the 1938 State lottery-loan were exchanged for a new, ' freely circulating ' 3 per per cent lottery-loan; 5 roubles of the older bonds were exchanged for 1 rouble in the new. All other bonds had to be exchanged in the proportion of 3: 1 for a new 2 per cent conversion loan which was issued in 1948.

1947 *uniform retail prices*

Rationing of food-stuffs and manufactured goods was abolished on 16th December 1947, and the Ministry of Trade was given the task of fixing ' uniform retail prices ' graded according to geographical area. These uniform prices were not to apply to kolkhoz trade nor to the sale of the goods which the co-operative organizations obtained for themselves.

For the three zones the following firm prices were fixed for bread and other foodstuffs (in roubles per kilo):

	Zone 1	Zone 2	Zone 3
Rye bread	2·80	3·00	3·20
Wheaten bread of 2nd-class flour	4.00	4·40	4·80
„ „ „ 1st-class „	6·20	7·00	7·80
Rye flour, sifted ..	4·40	4·80	5·20
Wheaten flour, 2nd class ..	5·70	6·20	7·00
„ „ 1st „ ..	7·00	8·00	9·00
Millet, crushed, 1st class ..	5·50	6·00	6·50
Buckwheat groats	11·00	12·00	13·00
Macaroni of flour, 1st class ..	9·00	10·00	11·00
Lump sugar, refined	13·50	15·00	16·50
Meat, bovine, medium-fat, 1st class	28·00	30·00	32·00
Butter, salt, best grade	62·00	64·00	66·00
Sunflower oil, refined, in bulk ..	28·00	30·00	32·00
Pike-perch, fresh frozen, 1st class	10·50	12·00	10·50
Herring, large from Caspian, salted in barrel	17·00	20·00	17·00
Salt, ground, No. 2	1·60	1·60	1·80
„ „ No. 3	1·40	1·40	1·60
Oats	2·20	2·50	2·80

Apples, milk and eggs had maximum and minimum prices fixed to allow for seasonal variation; these were, in roubles:

	Zone 1	Zone 2	Zone 3
Apples, 'Kandil', 1st class: per kilo	8·00–12·00	12·00–18·00	16·00–25·00
Milk, unskimmed: per litre ..	2·50 – 3·50	3·00 – 4·00	4·00 – 5·00
Eggs, fresh, 1st category: per 10 eggs ..	10·00–14·00	12·00–16·00	14·00–18·00

The zones were not the same for all types of goods. Thus, for example, Moscow and Leningrad were included in the 3rd zone for fruit, but in the 2nd zone for other foodstuffs. For all goods, the districts in the far north and far east were considered to be in Zone 3.

Uniform prices for all zones were fixed for the following goods:

		Roubles
Tea, Georgian, '*bachovyi*', 1st class ..	100 gr.	16·00
Coffee, roast, unground, 1st class	1 kilo	75·00
Beer, '*Zhigulevskoye*', in bottles	Per half-litre	7·00
Glass of milk in 100-gramme packages	1 kilo	20·00
Caviar, granular in jar, of sturgeon or sterlet, 1st class	1 kilo	400·00
Vodka, '*Moskovskaya*'	Per half-litre	60·00

For industrial goods two prices were fixed, one for the towns and one for the country:

		In roubles:	
	per	Towns	Country
Cotton, printed, 'Krap D', 60–62 cm. wide	metre	10·10	11·20
Satin 'Extra', mercerized, 60–63 cm. wide	,,	25·20	28·00
Flannel, 'mélange', 142 cm. ..	,,	108·00	120·00
'Boston' all-wool, 136 cm. ..	,,	450·00	510·00

	per	In roubles: Towns	Country
Crêpe de Chine, all silk, printed in 1, 2 or 3 colours, 92–94 cm. . .	„	137·00	151·75
Woman's dress of cotton, 'Kashmir' 170–171, of cotton 184, 'sherstianka' 199	each	77·00	86·00
Woman's dress, woollen, crêpe 'jacquard' 20	„	510·00	560·00
Man's suit, single-breasted, half-wool 38	„	430·00	450·00
Man's suit, single-breasted 'Boston 124'	„	1,400·00	1,500·00
Man's shoes with leather soles, black 'chevreau' R 4004 . .	pair	260·00	288·00
Woman's shoes, R 4114	„	260·00	288·00
Man's goloshes, rubber, ordinary	„	45·00	45·00
Felt boots (man's) undyed . .	„	195·00	216·00
Woman's jacket, half-wool, size 48	each	190·00	210·00
Woman's stockings, cotton . .	pair	7·00	7·50
Man's stockings, patterned, with artificial silk	„	17·00	19·00
Sewing cotton, reel, black or white	reel	1·75	1·75
Matches	box	0·20	0·20
Toilet soap 'family'	100 gr.	4·00	4·00
Household soap, best sort, 60%	400 gr.	5·20	5·20
Paraffin	litre	2·00	2·50
Cigarettes, 'Kazbek', best grade No. 3	25	6·30	6·30
Woman's comb, celluloid . .	each	4·00	4·00
Wrist watch, 'Zvezda' and 'Zif'	„	900·00	900·00
Gramophone, model PT 3 . .	„	900·00	900·00
Wireless receiver, 'Rekord', 5-valve	„	600·00	600·00

K

Price reductions since 1947

These State uniform prices, which were fixed in December 1947, have been considerably reduced since then.

An edict of April 1948 decreed a reduction in retail prices of 10 per cent for such things as 'Moskvich' motor-cars, sewing machines, 'Rekord' and 'Rodina' wireless receivers, 'Moskva' cameras, concertinas, opera-glasses, cigars and cigarettes, perfumes and cosmetics, primus cookers, electrical hot-plates and black caviar, of 12 per cent for pocket-watches and wrist-watches, of 15 per cent for sporting-guns, 20 per cent for bicycles, motorcycles, gramophones, certain fancy goods, plastic utility goods, vodka, liqueurs, wines, beer, non-alcoholic drinks and vitamin preparations.

On 28 February 1949 a fresh regulation was issued according to which State retail prices were to be reduced from 1st March 1949 by an average of: 10 per cent for bread, flour, groats, macaroni, biscuits, meat, cured meats, preserved meats, fish, fish products, butter, tobacco goods, woollen cloth, silk materials, furs, ornaments of metal, imitation leather, etc., household utensils of metal (eating-implements etc.), electrical articles (kettles, hotplates, irons, etc.), cameras and binoculars; 12 per cent for suits, overcoats, dresses and other ready-made woollen clothing, 15 per cent for strong wines, brandy and fruit-wines, blouses, dresses, etc. of silk, sewing cotton, silk stockings, leather shoes and shoes with fur linings, head-gear (hats and caps), fancy textile goods, embroidery work and motor-cycles; 20 per cent for feeding-stuffs, cheese, perfumery goods, made-to-measure clothing, household utensils etc. of plastic and celluloid, certain iron- and leathergoods, bicycles, wireless sets, pianos and concertinas, gramophone records, goldsmith's work and typewriters; 25 per cent for liqueurs and television sets; 28 per cent for vodka; 30 per cent for hay, salt, cement, gramophones and clocks.

In 1950 and 1951 fresh reductions of State retail prices were ordered, both coming into force on 1st March. On both occasions, as previously in 1949, restaurants, cafés and other eating-places were ordered to make corresponding reductions in their prices. The following is a comprehensive survey of the percentages by which prices were to be lowered in 1950 for the various groups of goods and for individual articles:

Bread and confectionery 25·9–30 per cent; flour 21–30 per cent; groats, rice and leguminous plants 12–20 per cent; macaroni and vermicelli 25 per cent; food concentrates (infants' foods, oat-preparations, maize flakes, etc.) 14·5–15·2 per cent; corn and fodder 20–25 per cent; meat and cured meats 24–35 per cent; (prime beef, pork, sausage, etc. 24 per cent, forcemeat 35 per cent); fish and fish-products 10–35 per cent; fats, cheese and dairy products 10–35 per cent (unskimmed milk, cream, vegetable oil 10 per cent, tinned milk and dried milk 15 per cent, cheese 15–20 per cent, household lard 18 per cent, dairy butter 30 per cent, margarine 35 per cent); eggs 15 per cent; egg-powder 20 per cent; sugar, pastries and groceries 8–50 per cent (toffees in bulk 8 per cent, tea 10 per cent, lump sugar 12 per cent, castor sugar 15 per cent, cocoa, cakes and tarts 16·7 per cent, jams, marmalade and jelly 25 per cent, fine salt and cooking-salt 40 per cent, unground salt 50 per cent); Vodka, liqueurs and wines 16·2–49 per cent; (brandy 25 per cent, table wines 35 per cent, strong wines and dessert wines on average 49 per cent); beer, aerated waters and soft drinks 16–30 per cent (drinks of natural juices and extracts 16 per cent, beer 30 per cent); fruit 15–30 per cent; potatoes and vegetables 10–35·7 per cent; (potatoes, beetroot, etc. 10 per cent, cabbage and carrots 14·7 per cent, deep-frozen vegetables 30–35·7 per cent); cloths 12–24 per cent (all-woollen cloths, half-woollen worsteds, cloths of half silk and artificial silk 12 per cent, cottons and linens 15 per cent, coarser woollens 24 per cent); ready-made clothing, knitted goods and headgear 10–35 per cent (ready-mades in half-silk or artificial silk 10 per cent, ready-mades in cotton 13 per cent, ready-mades in wool 19–22 per cent, cotton, silk and woollen stockings 15 per cent, sports caps all wool 35 per cent); shoes 10–25 per cent (rubber shoes for men and women 10 per cent, leather shoes, rubber shoes for children 15 per cent, cloth shoes and shoes of combined fabric and leather 20 per cent, felt shoes 25 per cent); fancy goods and jewellery 10–30 per cent; 'cultural goods' and toys 10–30 per cent (pianos, writing paper, rubber toys 10 per cent, wireless receivers 15 per cent, cameras and other photographic articles 20 per cent, gramophones 25 per cent); household utensils and goods 10–50 per cent (paraffin 10 per cent, incandescent lamps 11 per cent, knives of ordinary steel 12 per cent, glass services 15 per cent, services of porcelain or faience, articles of stainless steel and new silver, vacuum cleaners, paraffin cookers, primus stoves etc. 20 per cent, electric irons, locks 25 per cent, household soap 40 per cent, toilet soap 50 per cent); building materials and various industrial goods 10–40 per cent (bicycle tyres and inner tubes, footballs, tennis balls etc. 10 per cent, nails, cement, slates, roofing board, window glass, polishes, oil paints, wallpaper, bicycles and spare parts, wrist-watches, pocket-watches, playing-cards, cigarettes, tobacco and mahorka (a tobacco substitute) 20 per cent, motor-cycles and spare parts 20–25 per cent, matches 25 per cent).

The reductions in prices made on 1st March 1951 affected provisions and certain industrial goods, but not textiles and footwear. Prices were reduced by 10 per cent for fish and fishproducts, margarine, cheese, milk and milk preserves, glass, eggs, biscuits, cakes, tarts, vodka, liqueurs and brandy, tomato- and fruit-juices, perfumes, cigarettes and tobacco, glass services, wireless receivers, bicycles, motor-cycles, clocks, nails, constructional iron, cement, wallpaper, sewing machines, mincers, paraffin cookers, knives, locks, ironmongery, pots, irons, axes, spades, sickles, saddlemaker's goods and plastic goods. Prices were reduced by 15 per cent for bread, yeast, flour, groats, rice and podded fruits, corn and fodder, macaroni and concentrated foods, meat and preserved meats, dairy butter, soya beans, household and toilet soap and mahorka. Finally prices were reduced by 20 to 22 per cent for salt, furniture, chinaware, matches, paraffin, petrol, slates, roofing felt and window-glass.

Some prices in Moscow in 1949

To complete this account of the regulation of State prices during the years 1947–1951, here are some observations made during the visit of the Swedish Trade Union Council delegation to Moscow in April–May 1949.

In one store there were women's shoes for from about 50 to 500 roubles a pair and men's shoes in leather from 95 to 550 roubles. Cigarette prices varied between 1·80 roubles for 25 to 9 roubles for 20. An alarm clock cost between 50 and 60 roubles, a box camera 90, a bicycle from 850 to 1,100, a motor-cycle 3,400. Beef and mutton were to be had for 21·60 to 27 roubles a kilo, salt herring from 12·50 to 22·60, pickled herring for 10·40, cod for 7·60, castor sugar for 13·50, butter for 51 to 63, cheese was 34 to 50 roubles a kilo, and mandarin oranges were 1 rouble each.

The members of the delegation visited a kolkhoz market in Moscow on two consecutive days and made notes of the prices. It is difficult to judge to what extent those observations were representative for the time of year. The visits were made immediately before 1st May holiday, when the market is perhaps more than usually a seller's one, and no attempt was made to haggle about the price. Potatoes were offered for from 80 kopeks to 1·25 roubles a kilo, oranges for 6 to 10 roubles each, apples for 15 to 20 roubles a kilo, carrots for 4 to 5, sauerkraut for 3 to 5, sour cream for 25, meat and pork for 35 to 40 roubles per kilo. The price of milk rose from 4·50 roubles a litre on the first day to 5·50 on the second. When a couple of the delegates some days later visited a collective-farm outside Moscow they were told that the members were accustomed to sell milk for 1·50 roubles a litre in the nearby town of Zvenigorod.

Domestic production of foodstuffs

During and since the war large numbers of workers and employees have supplemented their victuals by growing vegetables in allotments provided by the concern for which they work. It was reckoned that in 1948 some 19 million workers and officials had individual or joint kitchen-gardens, and the crop of potatoes and vegetables was calculated at 758 kilos per grower.

Public places of refreshment

During the industrialization of the 1930's there was rapid expansion of ' the public provision of meals ', through the development of dining-rooms, buffets etc. as adjuncts to places of work. In 1937 the total turnover of State and cooperative places of refreshment was calculated at 10·2 milliard roubles, while the whole retail turnover amounted to 143·7 milliard. In 1940 the production of the public places of refreshment amounted to about 6 milliard helpings and their turnover corresponded to about 13 per cent of the total retail turnover.

In November 1947 the Ministry of Trade issued the following regulations on price-fixing for public places of refreshment.

Places of refreshment were divided into three categories, for each of which a different percentage was to be added to the costs; there were separate regulations for 'restaurants of higher class'.

To the 1st category belonged restaurants (other than those of the highest class) and their branches, cafés of higher class and buffets at State theatres.

To the 2nd category belonged dining-rooms with branches and buffets which did not receive free premises, light, fuel, water and transport, as well as teahouses, cafés (other than those of higher class), buffets at railway stations.

To the 3rd category belonged dining-rooms with branches and buffets serving workers, employees and students at concerns, institutions and educational establishments, which supplied them with free premises, light, fuel, water and transport; also in the 3rd category are dining-rooms for children and students at middle schools and trade schools.

At all places of public refreshment the prices of dishes were to be fixed by adding a certain percentage to 'the value of the raw materials'. If the raw materials were received from centralized State supplies or from the concern's or institution's own cultivation, their value was to be calculated according to the State retail prices. For agricultural products (other than bread-corn) purchased on the open market or obtained through 'decentralized' supplies, the value was to be calculated according to the actual cost plus special fixed additions (15 per cent for potatoes, vegetables, wild fruits and berries, 5 per cent for other products); the calculated raw material values were not however to exceed the State retail prices.

For places of refreshment in 1st, 2nd and 3rd categories, the maximum percentage which might be added to the value of the raw materials to make the price of the various groups of dishes was as follows:

	1st category	2nd category	3rd category
Group 1 ..	30	20	10
„ 2 ..	40	30	15
„ 3 ..	65	50	35
„ 4 ..	45	35	20
„ 5 ..	65	45	30
Caviar ..	10	10	5

Group 1 comprises ' delicatessen ' (sausage, cheese, ham, salmon, etc.) served without being heated or ' culinary treatment ', preserved meat and fish, boiled and baked eggs, milk, milk products, ice of own making.

Group 2 comprises cold meats, herring *au naturel*, omelettes, sausage, ham and other delicacies in helpings with garnishings and ' culinary treatment ', farinacious dishes (pancakes, pasties, etc.), sweets and puddings, berries, vegetables (cleaned and dressed, served in helpings or individually).

In *Group* 3 are the ' dinner-dishes ' (soups and hot dishes) of vegetables (without meat or fish), tinned vegetables, salads of gherkin, tomatoes, potatoes, provençal cabbage, radishes in sour cream, ' vinegrette '.

In *Group* 4 are the ' dinner-dishes ' (soups and hot dishes) of meat, fish, groats and such-like, and also hot drinks other than tea.

Group 5 consists of dishes served by the plateful (soups and hot dishes).

For higher quality restaurants the prices of dishes in Group 2 were to exceed those of 1st category eating-places by 10 per cent of the value of the raw materials, and for dishes in Groups 4 and 5 by 20 per cent of the value of the raw materials. In the case of early vegetables and early potatoes the extra was to be reckoned as a percentage of the price during the autumn and winter season.

Bread and pastries, cigarettes, tobacco and matches were to be sold at current retail prices. Soft drinks, confectionery and fruit were to be sold with an extra 20, 10 and 5 per cent respectively above the retail prices in 1st, 2nd and 3rd category places of refreshment. A glass of tea in 1st category places of refreshment was to cost 20 kopeks without sugar and 75 kopeks with sugar (using 0·5 grammes of tea and 25 grammes of sugar) and in 3rd category places 10 and 25 kopeks respectively (0·25 grammes of tea, 10 grammes sugar). Separate regulations were issued governing the prices of beer, wine and spirits.

Transport charges

Finally, here are some particulars about the charges for passenger transport and public services.

From 16th August 1948 there was a zone tariff in force for the railways. The following are some examples of the prices of tickets according to this tariff:

Cost of travel tickets, in roubles, including insurance charge

		Hard Coach:		Soft Coach:	
		Adult	Child	Adult	Child
Zone 1 –	5 km. ..	1·25	0·55	2·05	0·70
6 –	10 km. ..	1·75	0·65	3·45	0·95
96 –	100 km. ..	17·10	4·60	29·40	8·50
981 –	1020 km. ..	91·10	23·95	157·65	41·30
4901 –	5000 km. ..	265·55	68·30	462·90	117·60
9901 –	10040 km. ..	498·90	126·65	871·25	219·70

A child under 5 years old is allowed to accompany an adult free if it does not occupy a separate seat. Other children up to the age of 10 have to have children's tickets.

The following extra charges are made for reserved seats and sleepers and for express travel:

	Zone (kilometres)		
Hard coach	0–610	821–1060	9761–10320
Reserved seat	6·85	10·70	64·90
Sleeper: ordinary train ..	13·70	21·40	129·85
mail ,, ..	27·35	42·80	259·65
express ,, ..	30·70	53·05	379·80
Express travel surcharge:			
ordinary train ..	6·85	10·70	64·90
mail ,, ..	13·70	21·40	129·85
Soft coach			
Sleeper: ordinary train ..	20·60	32·10	194·80
mail ,, ..	41·15	64·15	389·60
express ,, ..	51·35	88·15	574·70
Express travel surcharge:			
ordinary train ..	10·30	16·05	97·40
mail ,, ..	20·60	32·10	194·80

Reserved seats cost as much for children as for adults. The surcharge for express travel for children is one-quarter of the extra charged for adults. Bedclothes (one pillow, two sheets and a handtowel) cost 15 roubles for 5 days. Tickets for through-sleepers have special prices.

16 kilos of hand baggage are allowed free for adults and 8 kilos for children (this does not include briefcases, women's handbags and such). Registered luggage is charged according to a separate tariff. When luggage is put into a left-luggage office its value has to be declared; the charge is 5 kopeks for every 100 roubles value.

The following are some examples of the fares for aeroplane and steamboat travel (roubles):

		Aeroplane from Moscow to		
Ticket:		Leningrad	Baku	Vladivostok
hard class	.. ..	185	450	1445
soft „	.. ..	240	495	1700
Transport of 1 kilo:				
baggage	.. ..	2·45	6·80	21·25
freight	.. ..	1·45	4·00	12·50

		Steamboat from Moscow to		
		Gorki	Saratov	Astrachan
With sleeper:		(896 km.)	(2229km.)	(3142 km.)
1st class	.. ..	146·90	235·90	294·20
2nd „	.. ..	111·00	177·10	220·80
3rd „	.. ..	76·20	120·70	150·30
Without reserved seat:				
3rd class	.. ..	51·90	83·30	103·50
4th „	.. ..	35·40	56·40	69·80
10 kilos baggage	..	4·74	6·36	7·40

Taxes for municipal services

The handbook *The Finance of Building- and Municipal Economies*, published in 1948, gives the following particulars about the charges made for certain municipal services.

Prior to 1948 the charges for municipal services varied very considerably. Thus, for example, a trip in a tramcar in Moscow, Leningrad and Kiev cost 15 kopeks, in Riga 20 kopeks and in Alma-Ata 30 kopeks. The average charge for electric current to households was 17 kopeks per kilowatt hour in Georgia and 1·83 roubles in Estonia. Laundry cost 1·10 roubles per kilo in Moscow and Leningrad and 4·16 roubles in the Moldavian Soviet Republic. The edict of 9th August 1948 issued by the Council of Ministers introduced the following uniform prices for municipal services:

Travel by underground railway: 50 kopeks per journey.

Travel by tramcar, irrespective of distance: 30 kopeks for a journey within the town, 50 kopeks on routes going outside the town limits, 1 rouble for transport of parcels.

Travel on buses or trolleycars: 15 kopeks per kilometre.

Electricity: 40 kopeks per kilowatt hour.

Gas: 20 kopeks per cubic metre.

Municipal baths: on the average, 1·50 roubles per bath.

Laundries: on an average, 2 roubles per kilo of dry washing.

The charges made at municipal baths and laundries vary round the average given in the regulation. Where the charge previously made was higher than that given in the regulations, it was to remain at the former level.

APPENDIX I

RULES AND REGULATIONS FOR THE TRADE UNION ORGANIZATIONS IN THE SOVIET UNION

ADOPTED AT THE 10TH ALL-UNION TRADE CONGRESS (27TH APRIL 1949)

UNDER the leadership of the Communist Party of the Soviet Union (the Bolsheviks) the Soviet people has built up a socialist society and is successfully fulfilling an historic task—the successive transition from socialism to communism. In the Soviet Union the exploiting classes have been entirely liquidated, the exploitation of one person by another has been abolished for all time, unemployment has been banished from the towns and poverty from the countryside, the material and cultural living standard of the workers has been raised considerably. Work, which under capitalism is a heavy burden, has in our country been transmuted into a point of honour, a thing of glory, courage and heroism. ' With us people do not work for exploiters, nor to enrich parasites, but for themselves, for their class, for their own soviet society, where the best persons in the workers' class wield the power ' (Stalin).

The historic successes of the workers of the Soviet Union are established in the Constitution of the Soviet Union.

The Constitution guarantees all citizens of the Soviet Union the right to work, the right to rest, the right to education, the right to material security in old age, sickness and loss of ability to work. Women in the Soviet Union enjoy the same rights as men in all spheres of economic, public, cultural, social and political life.

In the interest of the workers and in order to cement the socialist order of society, the law guarantees the citizens of the Soviet Union the right of free expression, liberty of the press, the right of assembly and the right to join together in social organizations.

In the Soviet Union the trade unions constitute a social nonparty mass organization and unite on a voluntary basis workers and employees in all occupations without distinction of race, nationality, sex or religious conviction.

The trade unions of the Soviet Union perform all their activities under the direction of the Communist Party—the organizing and directing power in the Soviet society. The trade unions in the Soviet Union gather the working masses round the party of Lenin and Stalin.

The trade unions endeavour by all means to strengthen the socialist state and its social order, the moral-political unity of the Soviet people, the fraternal co-operation and friendship between peoples in the Soviet Union; they take active part in the elections to the organs of State power; they organize workers and employees to fight for uninterrupted development of the national economy; are active in trying further to raise the material prosperity of the working-people and in every way to satisfy their cultural needs.

The trade unions educate their members in a spirit of Soviet patriotism and a communistic attitude to work and their socialist civic property; they work for a communistic education of the workers and towards the end that the workers may be raised to the cultural and technical level of the engineers and technicians; they strive to develop among their members a sense of proletarian internationalism, struggle for the unity of the international workers' movement, for lasting peace and democracy throughout the world. The trade unions are ' a training organization, an organization for recruiting and education, they constitute a school, a school for management, a school for economy, a school for communism ' (Lenin).

In the Soviet socialist order of society the State protects the rights of the working people and gives expression in its laws to the interests of the people. The trade unions co-operate actively in working out the laws concerning production, working conditions, living-standards and culture, and fight for consistent application of these laws.

The trade unions:

organize socialist competition among workers and employees to fulfil and exceed State plans, to raise the productivity of labour, to improve the quality and reduce the costs of production;

co-operate in the planning and regulation of wages for workers and employees and in the shaping of wage-systems guided by the socialist principle of payment in accordance with the quantity and quality of work, work for the establishment of new progressive performance norms, watch to see that work is credited and the piece-wage system and the progressive bonus system applied in the right manner;

help the workers and employees to increase their skill, propagate the experiences made by the pioneers among workers and employees, those who have broken new ground in production and science, co-operate to introduce advanced technical methods into industry;

conclude collective agreements with the managements of concerns;

exercise control of workers' protection and the safety arrangements of concerns and institutions; assist in the solution of labour conflicts; conclude agreements with the management of concerns on the use of grants for safety measures and workers' protection;

manage the State social insurance, fix and pay out assistance to workers and employees during temporary loss of working ability, work for a better organization of medical services for workers and health-care for women and children, found sanatoria and rest-homes, organize funds for mutual aid, assist in the allocation of dwelling space in the houses of concerns and institutions, exert a mass control over the implementation of plans for the construction of dwellings and of buildings for cultural and general purposes, of the work done in places of refreshment, in shops, general municipal enterprises and in the transport services of the towns;

help the members of the trade unions to enhance the level of their political and general education, propagate political and academic knowledge, conduct a comprehensive propaganda for the technique of production; establish clubs, houses and palaces of culture, red corners and libraries, work for widespread amateur artistic activity, for physical culture, sport and tourism among workers and employees;

co-operate in inducing women to take an increasing part in public life and skilled work, help workers and officials in the communistic rearing of their children;

represent the workers and officials before State and social organs on questions concerning conditions of life and work and of culture.

I—*Members of Trade Unions, their rights and obligations*

1. Every citizen of the Soviet Union who works in an enterprise or an institution or who studies at a higher establishment of learning, trade middle school or school for training craftsmen, can become a member of a trade union.

2. A member of a trade union *has a right*:

   (a) to take part in general meetings of the trade union members;

   (b) to elect and be elected to all union organs, union conferences and congresses;

   (c) to raise questions before a union organ and put proposals concerning the improvement of the functioning of the union;

   (d) at union meetings, conferences, congresses and in the press to criticize the union's local and superior organs and the actions of their functionaries and to address himself to all controlling union organs with questions, reports and complaints;

   (e) to apply to the union for protection and support for his rights in cases where the management of his concern has broken the collective agreement or the laws in force concerning labour questions, social insurance, cultural services and welfare arrangements;

   (f) to demand personally to be present on all occasions when the union organ makes a decision affecting his actions or behaviour.

3. A members of a trade union *is obliged*:

   (a) strictly to observe State discipline and labour discipline;

   (b) to guard and strengthen the socialist property of society as the sacred and inviolable foundation of the soviet system, the source of his country's riches and strength, the fountainhead of a life of well-being and culture for all workers;

   (c) to enhance his trade qualification (skill) and learn to master the technique of his job;

   (d) to observe the rules and regulations of his trade union and punctually to pay his membership dues.

4. A member of a trade union *has the following privileges*:

    (a) in accordance with the laws enacted, he receives assistance from the State social insurance funds but is paid more than those who are not members of a union;

    (b) he has priority for warrants for visits to rest-homes, sanatoria and health resorts, and also for his children to stay in crèches, kindergartens and pioneer camps;

    (c) in case of need he receives material help from trade union funds;

    (d) he enjoys free legal aid through the union's organ;

    (e) he has the right for himself and his family to use the union's cultural institutions and sports grounds on the conditions fixed by the union organ;

    (f) he has the right to become a member of the fund for mutual aid in his union.

5. Entry into a trade union takes place after personal application of the person wishing to join the union. The question of joining the union is decided at a meeting with a union group and confirmed by the union's departmental committee or, where there is no departmental committee, by the workshop-, factory-or house-committee. In union organizations that do not have trade groups, the decision on admittance is taken at a general meeting.

6. The seniority of a trade union member is reckoned from the day when the decision to admit him is taken at a meeting within a union group or trade union organization in his department, concern or institution. Those who have won entrance into a trade union receive a membership card through the union's factory-, workshop- or house-committee.

7. If a member of one union has transferred to a concern or an institution whose union organization belongs to another union, his membership is transferred to that union without payment of an entrance fee and he retains his union seniority.

8. The period spent by a member in the armed forces of the Soviet Union is reckoned in his trade union seniority.

9. When a trade union member, whether by reason of ill-health or old age, ceases to work and receives a pension, he has the right to remain in the union.

10. Workers and employees employed seasonally retain their trade union seniority if they take the work up again in the following season. Members of the artisans' co-operatives, *artels*, cannot at the same time be members of a trade union. If, prior to their joining the *artel*, they had been members of a union, their former union seniority is restored to them if they transfer back from an *artel* to a concern or institution.

11. Members of a union who have broken its rules, not paid their membership dues for more than three months or who have behaved in an undisciplined manner, can by decision of their union organ be adjudged the following punishments: warning, public rebuke, severe warning ('*vygovor*') and as an extreme measure expulsion from the union.

A decision to expel, which is taken at a meeting within a department or of a union group, comes into force once it has been confirmed by the union's factory-, workshop- or house-committee. The decision of a primary union organization to punish a member must be taken in his presence.

II—*The organization and structure of the trade unions*

12. The trade unions are constructed on the basis of democratic centralism, which involves the following:

(a) all union organs, from the lowest up, are elected by the union's members and are responsible to them;

(b) the union organizations decide all questions arising out of union work in accordance with the rules and regulations of the union and the decisions of their superior organs;

(c) the decisions of the union organizations require a majority of the members' votes;

(d) the inferior organs of a trade union are subordinate to the superior ones.

13. The trade unions are organized in accordance with the principle of production: all who work in an enterprise or an institution belong to the same trade union; each trade union embraces workers and employees occupied in one branch of the national economy.

14. To co-ordinate the activities of the trade unions in the provinces, areas and republics, union councils are set up in the various provinces, areas and republics.

15. The supreme controlling organ for each union organization is the general meeting (for the primary organizations), the conference (for regional, town, province, area and republic organizations), the congress (for the trade union).

By general meeting, conference or congress the respective committees (departmental, factory-, workshop-, house-, regional, town-, provincial, area-, republic-, central committee) are elected to be the executive organ and to conduct the current work of the whole organization.

16. All controlling organs of the trade unions, as also the delegates to the unions' conferences and congresses, are elected by secret ballot.

At the election of union organs the members of the unions have the right to nominate candidates, to oppose and criticize any of them.

The union organs elect chairman, secretary and council members from among their members by open vote.

17. Election to any trade organ whatever can be held prior to the time prescribed on the demand of at least two-thirds of the union members who are represented by that organ, or as the result of a decision of a superior union organ.

18. At general meetings of union members, union conferences and congresses, as at the meetings of the union committees and the union councils, there shall be considered to be a quorum if at least two-thirds of the members, or delegates or committee members, are present.

19. Union organs are bound to observe union democracy without deflection: to summon general meetings and conferences of the union members, to present reports and arrange elections, to create conditions for the development of criticism and self-criticism within the union organizations, to see that the union members take a predominant part in union work, arrange meeting with the active union cadres.

20. Commissions for the various kinds of union work are set up in

the union's departmental, factory-, workshop-, house-, regional, town-, provincial, and area-committees and in the union's council. In the All-Union Council and the unions' central committees, as well as in councils and committees of greater compass within republics, areas and provinces, departments and sectors are organized.

III—*The Superior Organs of the Trade Unions*

21. The supreme organ for trade unions in the Soviet Union is the All-Union Congress.

   The trade unions' All-Union Congress:

   (a) hears and accepts the reports of the unions' central councils and commissions of review;

   (b) makes rules and regulations for trade unions in the Soviet Union;

   (c) fixes the unions' current tasks, hears reports from central economic organs and lays down the lines for the unions' co-operation in the struggle to fulfil and exceed the national economic plans and to raise the material welfare, cultural and political level of workers and employees;

   (d) determines the rôle of the union organizations of the Soviet Union with the international trade union movement;

   (e) elects the All-Union Central Council and a commission of review.

22. The All-Union Congress of trade unions is called at least once every four years. The congress must be announced at least two months in advance.

23. In the intervals between All-Union Congresses the All-Union Central Council directs all activities of the trade unions.

24. The All-Union Central Council:

   (a) decides the current tasks of the trade unions in general and also special questions of union work;

   (b) co-operates in working out the plans of the national economy;

(c) directs socialist competition;

(d) acquaints itself with the reports from trade unions' committees, as well as with reports from Ministers and authorities concerning production, cultural measures and welfare arrangements for workers and employees;

(e) works out and submits to the Government draft legislation concerning wages, workers' protection, social insurance, cultural measures and welfare arrangements for workers; issues instructions, rules and explanations concerning the application of labour legislation in force;

(f) directs the administration of the State social insurance;

(g) carries out cultural, sport and other mass measures of an all-union character;

(h) organizes trade schools and courses;

(i) confirms the trade unions' budgets;

(k) represents the union organizations of the Soviet Union within the international trade union movement and takes part on their behalf in international trade union gatherings.

(l) has its printed organ—the paper *Trud*—the publishing house Profizdat, publishes periodicals, bulletins, etc.

25. The All-Union Central Council elects a presidium and a secretariat. Plenary meetings of the General Council are called regularly.

26. The supreme controlling organ for each trade union is the Congress of the Union. A union congress is summoned every other year. The delegates to the congress are elected by the union members at meetings and conferences in accordance with the procedure laid down by the union's central committee. The central committee must give information of the congress being summoned at least one month before.

Members of, and candidates for, the union's central committee and commission of review, who are not elected as delegates to the congress, have the right to speak at the congress but not to take part in its decisions.

The union congress acquaints itself with the reports of the central committee and commission of review, decides the union's current tasks, confirms its rules and regulations, acquaints itself with reports from economic organs concerning the fulfilment of the State plans, discusses questions concerning cultural measures and welfare arrangements for workers, matters concerning the international trade union movement, elects the union's central committee, commission of review and delegates to the All-Union Congress of Trade Unions.

If the All-Union Central Council or the union's central committee so decides, an extra congress can be called.

27. The union's central committee directs the entire activities of the union during the intervals between congresses.

The central committee and commission of review of a union are elected for a period of two years and are constituted as the congress decides.

28. The central committee of a trade union:

(a) organizes socialist competition, together with the economic organs judges the results of the all-union socialist competition, acquaints itself with their reports on the state of production, protection of workers and safety measures, organizes the conclusion of collective contracts and agreements concerning workers' protection, takes steps to improve the functioning of the concerns, institutions and union organizations in respect of the organization of work and the wage system, the promotion of socialist competition, social insurance, material welfare arrangements and cultural services for workers and employees;

(b) confirms the trade union's budget and the budget for the State social insurance and approves reports on their fulfilment;

(c) registers the collective contracts concluded by the local union organizations with the managements of concerns;

(d) fixes compulsory rules and norms for safety arrangements within its branch of production;

(e) organizes ideological and political education and instruction of the union cadres;

(f) publishes printed union matter (newspapers, periodicals, reports, etc.);

(g) engages active members of the union for work in State, soviet, economic and social organizations;

(h) fixes the composition of the union's central committee and approves the leaders for departments in the union's central committee;

(i) maintains and develops connections with trade organizations in foreign countries through the All-Union Central Council.

Plenary sessions of the union's central committee are summoned regularly.

The central committee elects a presidium to direct the daily work of the union; this consists of chairman, secretary and members.

The central committee of a trade union is answerable for its actions to the union congress and to the All-Union Central Council.

IV—*The Unions' organs in republics, areas, provinces, towns and regions*

29. Union councils and commissions of review for provinces, areas and republics are elected at the respective ' intermediate union conferences ' for a period of two years.

Delegates to ' intermediary union conferences ' are elected at meetings of union members at concerns, institutions and educational establishments whose union organizations are directly subordinated to the unions' central committees, and at union branch conferences for towns, regions, provinces, areas and republics.

30. The unions' provincial, area- and republican councils:

(a) execute measures affecting several unions at the same time;

(b) co-ordinate common measures taken by union organizations in that province, area or republic and intended to further socialist competition for fulfilment and exceeding of State plans by the concerns and for the further improvement of the material well-being and cultural services of workers and employees;

(c) give general publicity to the experiences of those who have broken fresh ground in union work;

(d) direct measures in the sphere of sport and culture which affect several unions.

Plenary sessions of the unions' councils are summoned regularly.

31. The trade unions' committees and commissions of review for the various republics, areas, provinces, railway districts, industrial areas, towns, regions are elected at conferences of the unions concerned, which are held once every other year.

The conferences receive reports from the committees and commissions of review, discuss questions concerning union work, the organization of work and production, cultural services and welfare arrangements for workers and clerks, elect the controlling union organs, delegates to the union congresses and the ' inter-union conferences '.

32. The committees direct the union organizations which belong to the trade union in question; organize the union organizations' execution of the decisions of the central council and of the unions' central committees within the various republics, areas, provinces, towns, regions, railway district or industrial areas; confirm the calculations of the unions' primary organizations; arrange meetings with the active union cadres. Full meetings of the committees are held regularly. For all their activities the committees are responsible to the appropriate conferences of union members in the republic, area, province, town, district and to the unions' central committees, and where measures carried out in republics, areas and provinces affecting more than one union are concerned, they are also responsible to the unions' councils.

33. The union councils and the committees elect from among their members a chairman, secretary and members of the presidium.

V—*The primary organizations of the unions*

34. The union's primary organizations are the basis of the union. The union's primary organizations consist of union members who work in an enterprise or an institution. The supreme organ for the union primary organization is the general meeting of members.

In enterprises and institutions where it is impossible to call a general meeting because of multiple shift-work or of large distances between different departments, shift-meetings are held or conferences of union members in the enterprise or institution.

35. The union primary organization has the following tasks:

(a) to mobilize all workers and employees in the enterprise or institution for fulfilling and exceeding the production plan, strengthening labour discipline and extending socialist competition;

(b) to prevail upon all workers and employees to become members of the trade union and to work for their political enlightenment;

(c) to fulfil its obligations in accordance with the collective agreement;

(d) to develop practical steps to increase labour productivity, to improve quality, to introduce economic calculation into production departments and teams, to reduce production costs and to increase the earning capacity of the enterprise; to arrange production conferences and supervise the application of steps decided upon; to co-operate in the carrying out of ideas for rationalization;

(e) to organize Stakhanovite schools, ' sponsorship ' on the part of cadre workers and engineers and technicians towards new workers, to arrange lectures and talks about modern working methods and in other ways to help workers and employees to fulfil and exceed the output norms and to enhance their skill;

(f) continually to endeavour to improve conditions of work and welfare arrangements for workers and employees;

(g) to satisfy the cultural needs of the workers and employees and to develop on a broad basis mass cultural work and athletic work at the concern or institution:

(h) to put into practice the decisions of the higher union organs and those of general meetings.

36. For the direction of current work a union primary organization consisting of at least 25 union members elect a factory-, workshop- or house-committee and a commission of review, and

an organization comprising less than 25 members elects a union organizer for one year.

The numbers of each factory-, workshop-, house-committee and commission of review are fixed by a general meeting or a conference of the union members.

The factory-, workshop-, house-committee concludes collective agreements with the management of the concern and organizes the masses' supervision of their implementation; it directs the work of the production conferences; promotes the masses' participation in invention and rationalization; works on cultural measures and welfare arrangements for workers and employees; decides the composition of the social insurance commissions and councils; calls general meetings and conferences; organizes the implementation of decisions taken by a superior union organ; attracts union members to active social work.

37. If the factory- or workshop-committee so decides, departmental committees are formed in the departments of the concern, and union bureaux are set up in the departments and management of institutions, if the local committee so decides; they are elected for one year.

The departmental committees and the union bureaux organize all the union work in the departments, are responsible for implementing the decisions taken by the factory-, workshop- and local committees and superior union organs, arrange meetings of workers and employees, form union groups and direct the work of the union group organizers.

38. The union groups are formed to enable better care to be taken of the union members working in a team, at a machine, set, department, etc.

At general meetings of the union groups, union group organizers are elected by open vote for a period of one year. To assist the group organizer the union groups elect from among themselves an insurance delegate and a social inspector for workers' protection.

The group organizer strives to get all workers to be members of the trade union, collects members' dues, organizes socialist competition and helps the factory-, workshop-, local, or departmental committee to carry out measures of cultural service and welfare arrangements for the workers and employees.

VI—*The trade unions' funds*

39. The trade unions' funds consist of entrance fees and monthly membership dues, income from institutions of culture, enlightenment and sport, from auxiliary enterprises, buildings and establishments and other receipts.

40. The monthly membership dues amount to one per cent of the actual monthly earnings and for students one per cent of their monthly stipendium. For trade union members who are pensioned and not working, or studying without a stipendium, the membership is one rouble a month.

41. The entrance fee paid on becoming a member of a union is one per cent of the wage received or stipendium, and for students not in receipt of a stipendium, one rouble.

42. The funds of the All-Union Central Council consist of payments made by the central committees of branch unions out of membership dues received, the amount being fixed by the Central Council, and of other receipts.

43. The union councils in republics, areas, districts and provinces are maintained out of the Central Council's funds in accordance with an approved scale.

44. The unions' funds are used for the cultural service of union members, to give them material assistance, and for the measures of economic organization which the union organs take. The use of these funds is decided annually by the central committees when fixing the budgets and by the Central Council when fixing the total budget of the trade unions.

The funds are used by the union organizations according to calculations fixed by a higher trade organ.

The All-Union Central Council, the central committees of the unions, the republican, area-, provincial, factory-, workshop- and local committees publish their financial reports for the information of the union members.

45. The commissions of review of the union organs elect from among themselves a chairman and secretary. The commissions of review examine the expenditure of the union budget, the budget for State social insurance, the correctness and efficiency of the use

made of funds and of the union organizations' property, the book-keeping and the accounts.

The commissions of review render reports on their activities to congresses, conferences and general meetings at the same time as the union organs.

VII—*The rights of union organs as juridical entities*

47. The unions' factory-, workshop-, local, town-, regional committees, the committees for railway districts and industrial areas, provincial, area, republican and central committees, as well as the All-Union Central Council and the unions' councils in republics, areas, provinces are persons in law. They have stamps and patterned seals which are authorised by the central committee of the respective unions and the All-Union Central Council.

48. Each branch union has its rules and regulations which give expression to the particular circumstances of the union and which conform to the rules and regulations for trade unions in the Soviet Union.

The rules and regulations of each trade union have to be registered with the All-Union Central Council.

APPENDIX II

NOTES

THE territory of the Soviet Union comprises sixteen republics, of which the largest is the Russian Socialist Federative Soviet Republic (RSFSR). The Union's republics embrace different types of territorial unit, like provinces (*oblast*), area or territory (*krai*), autonomous republics, autonomous provinces, national districts (*okrug*), regions (*rayon*), '*uyezdi*', '*volosti*', towns and villages. The provinces and territories are relatively large units; in the RSFSR there were in 1945 forty-five provinces and six territories. The provinces and territories embrace certain towns and regions which are subordinate administrative units, the latter in their turn perhaps being made up of several villages and lesser towns.

Soviets (councils) is the name given to the representative assemblies for the various territorial units (republic, province, region, town, village, etc.). The parliament of the Soviet Union, of the union republics and of the autonomous republics is called the ' supreme soviet '.

According to the Constitution of the Soviet Union the right to put up candidates for election to the soviets is restricted to 'social organizations and associations ', that is to say, to the organizations of the Communist party, of the trade unions, the co-operatives, the youth organizations and cultural associations.

The Communist party, which is the only political party allowed, is described in the Constitution as ' the controlling core in all the workers' organizations, social as well as state ' (by ' State organizations ' is meant, among others, the soviets). In *The Legal Code of the Soviet Union* the party's controlling position is characterized thus: 'The party directs the state organizations, not along with the soviets, but through the soviets '.

In the Soviet Union's Constitution of 1936 a distinction is made between two types of legislative act, that is between laws (*zakon*) and ukases (*ukaz*). Laws are adopted by the Supreme Soviet of the Soviet Union as well as by the supreme soviets of the Union republics and of the autonomous republics. Ukases are issued by the presidium of the supreme soviet concerned and come into force immediately; certain ukases require subsequent confirmation by the supreme soviet.

The various Union republics have separate 'law-books' (*kodeks*) codifying the legislation in the various spheres. We have referred here and there (for example on p. 12) to the 1922 labour code: the work meant is the labour code (*Kodeks zakonov o trude*) for the RSFSR, which has served as the model for similar codes in various Union republics. According to *The Labour Laws of the Soviet Union* the labour codes for the various republics differ only in unessential details.

Edicts (*postanovlenie, rasporazhenie*) are issued by the Council of Ministers of the Soviet Union, of the Union republics and of the autonomous republics (see below). On the basis of the laws, ukases and edicts in force, the separate ministries issue notifications (*prikaz*) and instructions. The All-Union Central Council issues instructions, rules and 'directives for putting into practice' concerned with labour legislation.

The government of the Soviet Union is the Council of Ministers (prior to 1946 the expression 'Council of People's Commissars' was used); the members of which are appointed by the Supreme Soviet or (during the intervals between meetings of the Supreme Soviet) by the Presidium of the Supreme Soviet. There are councils of ministers also in the Union republics and in the autonomous republics (see below). The other administrative units (provinces, regions, towns, etc.) have executive committees which are appointed by the soviet concerned.

In the Constitution all central, regional and local administrative organs are represented as organs of State power. The various executive organs are, in accordance with the principle of 'democratic centralism', subordinated on the one hand to the soviet concerned and on the other to the executive organs of larger administrative units. Thus, for example, the council of ministers in a Union republic is subordinate both to the supreme soviet of that republic and to the Council of Ministers of the Soviet Union. Similarly, the executive committee of a town is subordinate to the town soviet and to the executive committee of the region in which the town is situated or (in the case of larger towns) the executive committee of the province or the council of ministers of the republic.

Under the Council of Ministers of the Soviet Union come both the ' unional ' and the ' unional-republican ' ministries and authorities. Corresponding to the latter are the so-called 'unional-republican organs ' in the different Union republics. Besides these there are in the Union republics ' republican ' ministries and authorities for which there is no corresponding organ for the whole Soviet Union. Thus, for example, there is only one ministry for foreign trade for the whole Soviet Union (unional ministry), but there are ministries of finance both for the Soviet Union and for the different Union republics (unional-republican ministries) and ministries of social care only for the Union republics (republican ministries). The unional ministries and authorities deal with business that comes within the Union's competence. The unional-republican ministries and authorities for the Soviet Union issue general directives for the corresponding organs in the various Union republics.

There are various forms of administration and organization in the nationalized part of industry and commerce. Thus, for example, certain enterprises in State industry are directed by unional ministries, others by unional-republican or republican ministries. Within the ministries there are supervisory boards (*glavnoie upravlenie*) for the various branches of industry. These supervisory boards control the industrial working-units (enterprises) either directly or through trusts (*trest*) embracing several enterprises. These trusts are legal entities (that is to say that they can in their own names acquire property rights, assume obligations and plead in a court of law). The various enterprises and trusts have directives and plans worked out for their functioning by their superior authorities.

In the Soviet Union there are the following types of court of justice (*sud*): (1) People's courts (for smaller districts) appointed by direct election; (2) Courts for provinces, areas, autonomous provinces, etc. which are appointed by the relative soviets; (3) Supreme courts for the Soviet Union, Union republics and the autonomous republics, which are appointed by the supreme soviets concerned; (4) Special courts (military tribunals, line-courts for railway transport and shipping).

The people's courts are the first-instance courts, for example, for certain actions over labour law. Appeal against their judgments may be made to higher instances (for example, to a provincial court or supreme court).

According to the penal code in force the courts can inflict the following penalties (no account is taken here of certain military punishments):

The death penalty, which was declared to be abolished in 1947 in time of peace, was, by ukase dated 12th January 1950, reintroduced for ' traitors-to-their-country ', spies, damage-doers and saboteurs (*podryvniki-diversanti*).

Certain crimes that ' are a threat to the foundations of the Soviet system ' can be punished by the person concerned being declared the enemy of the working people, deprived of his citizenship and expelled from the Soviet Union.

Soviet citizens serving abroad who refuse to return to the Soviet Union when told are to be declared outlaws, which entails confiscation of their entire property and death by shooting if they should cross the frontier of the Soviet Union.

Sentence of imprisonment can be served either in prison or in ' corrective-labour' (*ispravitelno-trudovie raboti*) in camps, colonies, etc. (see below). For certain crimes the penalty is imprisonment up to 25 years.

For certain lesser crimes (for example truancy, *cf.* p. 88) the punishment is ' corrective-labour without deprivation of liberty ' (see below).

Banishment (*ssylka*) means that the person so sentenced is constrained to reside in a specified place for a certain time. Banishment can be combined with corrective labour.

Prohibition-to-reside (*vysylka*) means that the person so sentenced is for a certain time not allowed to reside in certain places.

Loss of rights (*porazhenie prav*) means that the person sentenced is for a certain time deprived of one or more of the following rights: active and passive election; the right to hold posts in social organizations which are filled by election; the right to hold State positions; the right to use honorific titles; parental rights; the right of pension. Loss of the right of pension can be adjudged for ' State offences ', for certain military crimes in peace-time, in conjunction with imprisonment for 'selfish crimes' (*korystne prestupleniya*) and also in conjunction with the confiscation of property.

The *Penal Code* cites the following 'kinds of punishment' (*vidy nakazaniya*) other than the above: dismissal from service; prohibition on exercising certain functions or certain trades; confiscation of property; damages; public rebuke; warning.

Certain 'administrative' and 'disciplinary' compulsory measures amount to the same thing as certain of the punishments just mentioned. The following observations are based partly on sources of older date than the preceding.

According to an edict issued in 1934 by the Central Executive Committee of the Soviet Union, there was attached to the People's Commissariat for Internal Business (NKVD, later the Ministry of the Interior, MVD) 'a separate conference' (*osoboye soveshchanie*), which was given power to decide in respect of persons who had been found socially dangerous whether they were to receive residential prohibition (*vysylka*) up to 5 years, banishment (*ssylka*) for a maximum of 5 years, internment with corrective labour not exceeding 5 years, and (where foreigners were concerned) expulsion from the Soviet Union. At the end of an account of this edict in *Administrative Law* (published in 1946) the following is stated: ' Those who have been sentenced to residential prohibition or banishment have the right to take work with State, co-operative and social organizations and enterprises, in so far as that is not forbidden by law '. According to the same source those persons against whom an administrative order of residential prohibition or banishment has been issued and who are not fit to work are to receive assistance out of State funds.

In his *Concept of Crime* (*Ponatie prestupleniya*, Moscow, 1948) Professor N. Durmanov points out that punishment for crime can be inflicted by another authority than that prescribed in the laws on criminal procedure. In this connection he quotes a regulation of 1935 according to which infringement of the rules for entry and sojourn in the frontier districts was to be punished with internment in a camp for 1–3 years according to the decision of a special 'conference' with the People's Commissar for Internal Affairs. A regulation of 1937 made this the concern of the people's court.

According to *Penal Law* (Moscow, 1948), corrective labour without loss of liberty may be inflicted by administrative order (that is to say, by other organ than a court) for a period not exceeding one month.

Corrective labour without loss of liberty may, according to the same source, be performed either at the person's normal place of work or in work organized by the collective labour organ; work of this latter kind is, like the corrective establishments (camps, colonies, etc.), controlled by the Ministry of the Interior. When corrective labour is performed at the person's normal place of work, a maximum of 25 per cent is to be deducted from that person's income (that is to say, from the wages of a worker or employee, from the earnings from 'day-work' of a collective-farmer).

There are certain restrictions of social benefits involved when a person is performing corrective labour at his place of work (*cf.* pp. 113 and 120).

Separate regulations have been issued concerning the working conditions for those performing corrective labour with loss of liberty. According to the 1933 law on corrective labour for the RSFSR (*Ispravitelno-trudovoi kodeks RSFSR*), remuneration for the work performed is to be made in accordance with the instructions drawn up by the People's Commissariat for Judicial Affairs and the All-Union Central Council. Productive work was as a rule to be organized as piece-work. The conditions of work were to be fixed to agree with the general rules in the labour code for the RSFSR concerning hours of work, rest, work of women and young persons and workers' protection; the People's Commissariat for Judicial Affairs could, however, in consultation with the All-Union Central Council order exceptions from these rules. The law mentions different types of colonies for corrective labour, such as factory- and workshop-colonies, agricultural colonies and colonies for ' mass labour '. In his *About Soviet Justice* (Moscow, 1939) A. Vishinsky mentions as examples of the results of corrective labour such things as the construction of the White Sea canal and the Moscow-Volga canal, and also a number of factories and workshops.

Chapter 20 of *Penal Code of the Soviet Union* (published 1950), dealing with ' Offences in the sphere of labour relations ' gives the rules for sentences for 'truancy' and 'arbitrary leaving', and also certain other rules, a brief account of which now follows.

It is laid down in the ukase of 26 June 1940 that 'arbitrarily leaving' a position in a State, co-operative or social undertaking or institution is to be punished with 2–4 months' imprisonment and 'truancy' with up to 6 months' corrective labour at the person's place of work (cf. Chapter VIII). It is further laid down that directors of enterprises and heads of institutions are liable to be punished if they (a) neglect to take legal proceedings against those who have been guilty of arbitrarily leaving the enterprise or institution or of absenteeism without adequate reason, or (b) engage persons who have arbitrarily left their work at an enterprise or institution and who are trying to avoid punishment. The ukase gives no rules for the sentences to be given for these offences. According to *Penal Code of the Soviet Union* the director or head concerned should be sentenced as for 'crime in service', for example according to 109§, 111§ or 112§, par. 2, in the penal code for the RSFSR. According to these, the sentences would be respectively: imprisonment for at least 6 months (109§); imprisonment up to 3 years (111§); corrective labour of up to one month or dismissal, prohibition from occupying a controlling position for 2 years, damages or public rebuke (112§, par. 2).

According to 133§ in the penal code for the RSFSR, an employer (that is to say, a private individual or the person concerned in a State or social institution or enterprise) who infringes laws governing the use of manpower or laws on workers' protection and social insurance shall be sentenced to corrective labour of up to 6 months or a fine of up to 300 roubles. If the offence affects a group of at least 3 workers and if it is similar in character for all persons in the group and has been committed against them all simultaneously, the person in question shall be sentenced to imprisonment or corrective labour for a period of up to 1 year or to a fine of up to 10,000 roubles. If a person, in contravention of the rules for workers' protection, puts a wage-earner to work in such conditions that he loses, or could lose, his ability to work, he shall be sentenced to imprisonment for a period of up to 2 years or to corrective labour for up to 1 year or to fines up to 500 roubles. Anyone infringing such rules for workers' protection, safety regulations and rules for occupational hygiene as have been laid down by the local authorities in valid orders or through edicts, proclamations or instructions from the People's Commissariat for Labour (since 1933 from the All-Union Central Council) can have up to one month's corrective labour or a fine of up to 100 roubles imposed upon him by administrative order. According to a codicil added to 133§ in 1949, anyone who refuses to engage a pregnant woman because of her condition, or refuses to engage nursing-mothers or reduces their wages because of that circumstance, shall be sentenced to corrective labour of up to 6 months or to a fine of up to 1,000 roubles. If the offence is repeated, the punishment may be increased to imprisonment for up to 2 years.

108§ in the penal code of the RSFSR contains rules for the punishments to be inflicted for infringements of technical regulations, protective rules, etc. for building work, in the mining industry and in production departments where there is risk of explosion.

The following statements are taken from two articles by Professor V. M. Dogadov (' Stages in the development of the soviet collective agreement ' and ' On the subject of the soviet collective agreement and its validity '):

The obligations assumed in a collective agreement—by the management of the concern, the union organization and the individual wage-earner—are first and foremost of ' social, moral-political character '. The director of a concern has a general legal duty to manage the concern in such a way that the economic plan can be achieved and exceeded. This general duty is formulated in the collective agreement, in that the director of the concern is bound to take certain concrete steps, the purpose of which is the achievement and surpassing of the plan.

Failure by the director of a concern to fulfil his obligations according to the collective agreement can involve either (1) disciplinary responsibility (that is to say a superior organ imposes disciplinary punishment, which can mean that the director of the concern is dismissed his post); or (2) administrative responsibility (thus, for example, the labour inspector can intervene if the director of the concern neglects to take measures for the protection of his workers (*cf*. p. 83); or (3) criminal responsibility according to 134§ of the penal code for the RSFSR and corresponding paragraphs in the penal codes of the other union republics (the punishment for infringement of a collective agreement 'with criminal intent' (*zlonamerenno*) on the part of the 'employer' is imprisonment or corrective labour for up to one year or a fine of up to 10,000 roubles).

The obligations of the trade union organizations under a collective agreement are purely social and moral-political in character; no legal sanctions are incurred if these obligations are neglected.

If an individual wage-earner does not fulfil his obligations under the collective agreement (for example, to make full use of his working-time, to achieve his output norms and to take care of the property of the concern), this carries with it legal responsibility only if the wage-earner in question simultaneously infringes some 'legislative norm'; thus, for example, criminal responsibility attaches in cases of truancy, not because under the collective agreement the wage-earner is bound to 'give a full measure of working time', but because criminal responsibility is prescribed for that under the ukase of 26 June 1940 (*cf.* p. 88).

The present collective agreements contain, as well as concrete obligations for the management of the concern, the union organizations and the individual wage-earners, a few 'normative' stipulations which are intended to regulate working conditions for those employed by the concern in question (*cf.* p. 37). A number of 'normative' stipulations which are promulgated by State organs (for example 'tariff nets' for fixing wages, scales for progressive piece-work increments, etc.) are usually incorporated in the collective agreement, whereby the regulations become known to those employed at the concern in question; the legal validity of the regulations does not depend on the fact of their inclusion in the collective agreement.

According to a ukase of 28 December 1940 pupils at trade schools for 'labour reserves' (*cf.* p. 45) who arbitrarily leave the school, or by reason of systematic and heinous infringements of school discipline are excluded from the school, shall be sentenced to internment in a labour colony for up to one year. In *Problems of the Labour Laws* V. M. Dogadov stated that entry into the trade schools remained voluntary during the war as in time of peace and that the Council of People's Commissars had declared during the war that to omit to report for instruction after being summoned (*prizyv*) to a craft-, railway-, factory- or workshop-school, would only entail 'social action' (*obshchestvennoye vozdeistvie*). Criminal responsibility is incurred, according to Dogadov, only when a person who, after being summoned, reports for instruction, but later remains absent.

There now follows some further information about the Five-Year Plan 1946–1950 and some statistics to complete those already given in the text.

According to the Five-Year Plan the number of workers and employees was to reach 33·5 million by 1950. The Central Statistical Office reported 39·2 million workers and employees at the end of 1950.

By 1950 the total volume of industrial production, according to the plan, was to be 48 per cent more than that of 1940; the reported increase was 73 per cent.

The following are some statistics for industrial production in 1950:

Metal industry: 19·5 million tons of pig-iron, 25·4 million tons of steel, 17·8 million tons of rolled iron.

Fuel and power: 250 million tons of coal, 35·4 million tons of petroleum, 82 milliard kilowatt-hours of electrical energy.

Timber and building material: 280 million cubic metres of cut timber; 39 million cubic metres of sawn timber, 10·5 million tons of cement, 80 million square metres of window-glass.

Textile and light industries: 4,686 million metres of cotton material, 159·4 million metres of woollen material, 240 million pairs of leather footgear, 88·6 million pairs of rubber shoes, 580 million pairs of stockings.

Victuals: 1,300,000 tons of meat, 275,000 tons of animal fats, 880,000 tons of vegetable fats, 2,200,000 tons of fish, 2,400,000 tons of sugar, 19,000,000 tons of flour (these figures refer only to the industrial production).

According to the report of the Central Statistical Office, the planned figures were exceeded in 1950 in respect of steel, rolled iron, coal, petroleum and electrical energy. In light industry (textiles, ready-made clothing, knitted goods, shoe industry and others) production for 1950 was 17 per cent greater than in 1940;

the aims of the Five-Year Plan were not achieved in cotton-materials and footwear. From 1945 to 1950 the production of cotton materials increased 2·4 times, that of woollen goods 2·9 times, of leather footgear 3·2 and of rubber shoes 7 times. In the foodstuffs industries the production for 1950 exceeded the pre-war level by the following percentages: animal fats 57, vegetable fats 10, meat 7, fish 27, sausage 20, tinned goods 48, sugar 17, confectionery 23, soap and soft soap 16.

In agriculture it was planned that the 1950 harvest of corn should amount to 127 million tons, of sugar beet to 26 million tons, of raw cotton to 3·1 million tons, of flax fibres to 800,000 tons, and of sunflower seeds to 3·7 million tons. The Central Statistical Office reported for 1950 a ' gross harvest ' of circa 123 million tons of corn and 3·75 million tons of cotton.

The reported head of cattle at the end of 1950 (in the possession of all categories of owners, that is, individual collective-farmers and other private persons as well as *kolkhozes* and *sovkhozes*) was 57·2 (according to the plan, 65·3) million bovines, of which 24·2 million were cows, 24·1 (31·2) million pigs, 99 (121·5) million sheep and goats, 13·7 (15·3) million horses. For the sake of comparison, it can be mentioned that the head of cattle in July 1938 (within the pre-war boundaries of the Soviet Union), according to the Great Soviet Encyclopædia, amounted to 63·2 million bovines, 30·6 million pigs, 102·5 million sheep and goats, and 17·5 million horses. The same source gives the stock-breeding industry's ' gross production ' of meat as 3,607,000 tons (of which 1,564,000 tons were pork and bacon), of milk 28,861,000 tons and of wool 133,000 tons.

[Notes to pp. 131–132. According to Veselovsky, the ' stock of dwellings in the towns ' (*zhiloi fond v gorodakh*) at the end of 1926 was 159 million square metres of ' dwelling surface ', and the dwelling surface per inhabitant in ' urban communities ' (*v gorodskikh poseleniyakh*) 5·85 square metres; at the beginning of 1933 the corresponding figure for the total dwelling surface according to Veselovsky was 195 million square metres. In the *Draft for the second five-year plan*, under the heading 'Dwelling economy in the towns ', the total area at the end of 1932 was given as 185 million square metres, the population of the towns as 38·7 millions and the dwelling surface per inhabitant 4·78 square metres. The report on population statistics includes in the 'population of towns' residents in workers' communities and 'health resort communities'. I have not been able to check whether the figure Veselovsky gives for 'stock of dwellings in the towns' for 1939 (225 million square metres), which is based on a 'carry-forward' of the 1926 estimate (adjusted for new construction and loss through demolition, fire, etc.), takes in exactly the same areas as the figure for 'population of towns' in 1939 census (55·9 million); if it does, then the dwelling surface per inhabitant of towns and urban communities would work out at about 4 square metres. According to Zaslavsky, the dwelling area in towns at the time of the entry of the Soviet Union into the Second World War was about 254 million square metres; from the context, it would appear that that figure referred to the pre-war frontiers.

APPENDIX III

Sources

THE figures in italics at the end of the references to certain statements in the text, refer to the list of sources on pp. 186–193.

References in the text to *The Labour Laws of the Soviet Union* refer to the textbook that was published in 1949 (No. 38 in the list of sources). Chapters III–VIII and X follow this fairly closely.

References to the text

Chapter I—Page 12, 1922 Labour Code. *4.*— Page 13, private craft: *32*; censuses of 1926 and 1939: *62, 67.*— Page 14, particulars of the numbers of workers and employees assembled by Baykov (*66*) from official sources. Corresponding figures for the end of 1940 come from the report on the achievement of the Five-Year Plan 1946–1950 (*63*).—Page 15, the reports of the Central Statistical Office on the economic development during various years have been published in, among other sources, *Izvestia* (18/1/1948; 20/1/1949; 18/1/1950) and *Pravda* (26/1/1951) and quoted in *Narodnoie khoziastvo* (*68*).—Pages 15–16, measures against over-mobility 1930: *19, 20.*—Page 16, edict 1932: *21*; edict 1938: *8.*—Pages 17–18, ukases of 26 June, 2 October and 19 October 1940: *11.*—Pages 18–19, Labour legislation during the war: *41*; Five-Year Plan 1946–1950: *22.*

Chapter II. Reference is made to the following sources: *Rules and Regulations for the Trade Union Organizations* (*53*); *The Labour Laws of the Soviet Union* (*38*); Kuznetsov's report on the activities of the central council (*52*), *Trud* 15/2/1951.—Page 20: membership of the trade unions: *52, 62*; Page 23, Shvernik on the collective agreement: *36.*—Pages 24–25, instructions for wage commissions: *12.*—Page 28, funds for mutual aid: *12.*—Pages 29–30, edict on collective agreements for 1949: *12.*—Page 31, collective agreement for ' Stalin ' motor-car factory: *38.*—Pages

31–32, collective agreement for locomotive workshops in Kolomna: *54*.—'*Professionalny soyuz*' or '*profsoyuz*' has been translated as trade union organization or trade union.

Chapter III.—Largely based on *The Labour Laws of the Soviet Union* (*38*).—Pages 35–36, regulations on duty to work: *5*.—Pages 44–45, organization of the educational system: *65*; statistics: *68*.—Pages 45–46, labour reserves: *16*.—Page 46, rules for recruiting pupils to trade schools: *29*; Mochova's article: *72*. ' Komsomol ' is the name of the communist youth organization.

Chapter IV. This mainly follows *The Labour Laws of the Soviet Union* (*38*).

Chapter V. The account of the general principles for fixing wages (pp. 53–67) mainly follows *The Labour Laws of the Soviet Union* (*38*).—Pages 53–54, first section: *40*.—Page 54, dear-times increment 1946: *13*, *71*.—Page 55, extract from the tariff-qualifications handbook: *73*.—Pages 56, 58 and 67, agreement for locomotive workshop in Kolomna: *54*. The figures in the table on page 56 have been made to the nearest ten kopeks (1 rouble = 100 kopeks).—Page 58, lines 1–14: *55*.—Page 59: Anna Kuznetsova's autobiography: *59*; Manevich's article: *71*.—Pages 61–62, bonuses: *56*.—Page 62, prizes in socialist competition: *37*.—Pages 67–75, wages for workers and employees in the coal industry: *13*.—Page 75, wages in municipal undertakings: *47*.—Page 76, wages in retail trade: *50*.—Pages 77–78, wages in places of public refreshment: *51*.—Pages 78–80, wages for teachers: *14*.

Chapters VI–VIII. Mainly follow *The Labour Laws of the Soviet Union* (*38*). Page 86, model rules for internal ordering of work: *12*.—Pages 88–89, decisions in supreme court 1943: *5*; guiding edict from supreme court: *43*.—Page 94, quotation from Pasherstnik: *40*.

Chapter IX. Page 97, 1949 budget: *24*; 1950 budget: *34*; 1951 budget: *25*. Page 98, Zverev's report: *25*.—Pages 98–104, taxes and dues: *32*.—Page 104, Plotnikov: *33*; edict on the State loan 1949: Vechernaya Moskva 4/5/1949.—Page 105, *Incomes in the Soviet Union's State Budget*: *31*; pledging of bonds: *30*.

Chapter X. Page 106, 1949 budget: *24*; statistics for 1949: *Narodnoie khozhaistvo* No. 3 (*68*).—Pages 106–107, Zverev's report: *Narodnoie khozhaistvo* No. 4 (*68*); edict on fees at certain educational establishments: *15*.—Pages 107–108, stipendia: *14*; medical attention: *29*.—Page 109, medical attention in Moscow: *60*.—Pages 110–111, social care: *29*, *30*; financing: *57*; budget for social insurance 1949: the figures for the divisions were given at an exhibition arranged in connection with the All-Union Trade Union Congress in Moscow 1949.—Pages 112–125, account of the forms of help given by social insurance based on *The Labour Laws of the Soviet Union* (*38*), *State Social Insurance* (*17*) and articles in periodicals (*74, 75*).—Pages 126–127, benefit to those with large families and lone mothers: *2*.—Pages 127–129, crèches and kindergartens: *17*.—Pages 129–130, pioneer camps: *38, 52*.

Chapter XI. Page 131, dwelling statistics: *45, 18*.—Pages 132 to 139, legislation on rented dwellings: *18, 46*.—Pages 139–140, own-home building: *3, 12*.

Chapter XII. Page 141, organization of retail trade: *49*.—Page 142, regulation of retail prices: *49*.—Pages 142–143, monetary reform of 1947: *23*.—Pages 143–145, uniform retail prices of 1947: *Pravda* 15/12/1947.—Page 146, edict on price reductions: *Izvestia* 10/4/1948 and 1/3/1949, *Pravda* 1/3/1950, *Izvestia* 1-3-1951.—Page 149; domestic production of victuals: Kuznetsov (*52*), particulars from the exhibition mentioned in note to page 112.—Pages 149–152, places of public refreshment: *51, 58*.—Pages 152–154, fares for passenger transport: *61*.

Appendix I. Rules and regulations for the Trade Union Organizations: *53*.

Appendix II. Pages 171–173, legislation, administration and legal system: *26, 27, 28, 29*.—Pages 174–175, Penal Code: *6, 42, 43*.—Page 175, edict 1934: *7, 28*; edicts 1935 and 1937: *6, 44*.—Page 176, corrective labour: *10, 42, 64*.—Pages 176–177, penalties for labour crimes: *6, 43*.—Pages 178–179, Dogadov's articles: *69, 70*.—Page 179, ukase of 28 December 1940: *6*.—Pages 180 to 182, Five-Year Plan, statistics: *22, 45, 48, 62, 63, 76, 77*.

LIST OF SOURCES

(published in Moscow unless otherwise stated)

1. *Konstitutsiya (osnovnoi zakon) SSSR. Konstitutsii (osnovnye zakony) soyuznych sovetskikh sotsialisticheskikh respublik.* 1951. —The Constitution of the Soviet Union. The Constitutions of the Union republics.

2. *Kodeks zakonov o brake, semye i opeke RSFSR.* 1950.—Book of laws concerning marriage, family and guardianship for RSFSR. Official text with alterations to 1 July 1950 and appendices.

3. *Grazhdanski kodeks RSFSR.* 1950. — Civil code for the RSFSR. Official text with emendations to 1 July 1950 and appendices.

4. *Kodeks zakonov o trude RSFSR.* 1937.—Labour code for RSFSR. Official text with emendations to 1 July 1937 and appendices.

5. N. G. Alexandrov, E. I. Astrakhan, S. S. Karinsky, G. K. Moskalenko: *Zakonodatelstvo o trude.* 1947. Labour legislation. Text and commentary on labour legislation for the Soviet Union and the labour code for RSFSR.

6. *Ugolovnii kodeks RSFSR.* 1950.—Penal code for RSFSR. Official text with emendations to 1 July 1950 and appendices.

7. *Sobranie zakonov i rasporzhahenii Rabotzhe-krestianskogo pravitelstva SSSR.*—Collection of laws and government edicts. Volume for 1935.

8. *Sobranie postanovlenii i rasporzhahenii pravitelstva SSSR.*— Collection of government edicts. Volume for 1939.

9. *Sbornik zakonov SSSR i ukazov prezidiuma verchovnogo soveta SSSR.*—Collection of laws of the Soviet Union and of ukases of the Presidium of the Supreme Soviet of the Soviet Union. Years 1948–1950.

10. *Chronologicheskoye sobranie zakonov RSFSR. T. IX.* 1941.—
Chronological collection of laws for RSFSR. Part IX. Contains the text of the corrective labour code for the RSFSR (*Ispravitelno-trudovoi kodeks RSFSR*).

11. *Spravochnik po zakonodatelstvu dlya rabotnikov gosudarstvennoi promyshlennosti SSSR.* 1951.—Handbook of legislation for officials in the State industries of the Soviet Union. Contains the text of laws, edicts and other normative acts which had come into force prior to 1 September 1950.

12. *Spravochnik profsoyuznogo rabotnika.* 1949.—Handbook for trade union functionaries. Text of statutes, directives, etc. concerning conditions of work and the activities of the trade union organizations.

13. *Spravochnik po trudu i zarabotnoi plate dlya rabotnikov ugolnoi promyshlennosti vostochnykh rayonov SSSR.* 1948.—Handbook of working conditions and wages for officials of the coal industry in the eastern districts of the Soviet Union. Contains regulations governing working conditions and wages in force at 1 January 1948. Editor: V. Buchnev.

14. *Spravochnik meditsinskogo rabotnika po voprosam truda i zarabotnoi plati.* 1950.—Handbook for officers of the medical service for matters of wages and working conditions. Contains the text of laws, edicts and other normative acts. Editor: F. A. Artemjev.

15. *Vysshaya shkola.* 1945.—The higher school. Contains the text of edicts, proclamations and instructions. Editor: A. M. Chodzjajev.

16. *Trudovye rezervy SSSR.* 1950.—The Soviet Union's labour reserves. Contains the text of the laws, edicts and other normative acts in force at 1 March 1950. Editor: M. S. Rozofanov.

17. *Gosudarstvennoye sotsialnoye strachovanie.* 1948.—State social insurance. A collection of ukases, edicts, instructions and explanations.

18. *Zhilichnoye zakonodatelstvo.* 1950. Housing laws. A collection of laws, edicts, etc. in force 1 November 1950. Editor: P. I. Kudriavtsev.

19. S. Livsits: *Rabochye kadri*. 1931.—Worker-cadres. The train-ing and placing of qualified labour, etc.

20. Z. Morduchovich (Mochov): *Na borbu s tekushchtei rabochei siloi*. 1931.—To combat the over-mobility of labour. Contains certain material about the labour market.

21. *Borba za sotsialisticheskuyu trudovuyu disciplinu*. 1933.—The struggle for a socialist labour discipline. Contains the text of the Central Executive Committee and the Council of People's Commissars' edict of 15 November 1932 ' on dismissal for truancy and other sufficient causes '.

22. *Zasedaniya verchovnogo soveta SSSR (pervaya sessiya)*. 1946. —Meetings of the Supreme Soviet of the Soviet Union (first session). Shorthand report. Contains the text of the ' Law for the Five-Year Plan for reconstruction and development of the national economy of the Soviet Union 1946–1950 '.

23. *Postanovlenie soveta ministrov SSSR i Ts VKP (b) o provedenii denezhnoi reformi i otmene kartochek na prodovolstvennie i promyshlennie tovari*. 1947. Edict by the Soviet Union's Council of Ministers and the Central Committee of the Com-munist party on the implementation of monetary reform and the abolition of cards for foodstuffs and manufactured goods.

24. *Zasedaniya verchovnogo soveta SSSR (pyataya sessiya) 10–14 marta 1949 g*. 1949.—Meeting of the Supreme Soviet of the Soviet Union 10–14 March 1949 (fifth session). Contains a shorthand report of the debate on the budget for 1949.

25. *O gosudarstvennom budzete SSSR na 1951 god*. 1951.—On the Soviet Union's State budget for 1951. Speech of the Finance Minister, A. G. Zverev, plus the text of the law for the State budget for 1951.

26. *Osnovy sovetskogo gosudarstva i prava*, 1947. Bases of the Soviet Union's State and law. Textbook for non-juridical establishments of higher education. Editors: I. D. Levin and A. V. Karass.

27. *Sovetskoye gosudarstvennoye pravo.* 1948.—The legal code of the Soviet Union. Textbook for juridical institutes and juridical faculties. Contributors: A. A. Askerov, N. D. Durmanov, M. P. Kareva, V. F. Kotok, I. D. Levin, I. P. Trainin.

28. I. I. Evtichiev, V. A. Vlasov: *Administrativnoye pravo SSSR.* 1946.—Administrative law of the Soviet Union. Textbook for juridical institutes and faculties.

29. S. S. Studenikin, V. A. Vlasov, I. I. Evtichiev: *Sovetskoye administrativnoye pravo.* 1950.—Administrative law of the Soviet Union. Textbook for higher law schools.

30. *Finansovoye pravo.* 1946.—Fiscal law. Textbook for the juridical institute. Edited by N. N. Rovinsky.

31. *Dokhody gosudarstvennogo budzeta SSSR.* 1945.—Incomes in the State budget of the Soviet Union. Textbook for financial-economic institutes. Edited by A. K. Suchkov.

32. *Spravochnik nalogovogo rabotnika.* 1949.—Handbook for officers in the taxation service. Edited by D. V. Burmistrov.

33. K. N. Plotnikov: *Budzet sotsialisticheskogo gosudarstva.* 1948. —The budget of the socialist state. Historical account.

34. V. V. Lavrov: *Budzet strani sotsializma.* 1950.—Budget of the land of socialism.

35. *Sovetskoye trudovoye pravo.* 1939.—Labour Laws of the Soviet Union. Textbook for higher juridical studies. Edited by K. P. Gorshenin, R. P. Orlov, V. M. Dogadov, Y. A. Karasev.

36. *Sovetskoye trudovoye pravo.* 1946.—Labour Laws of the Soviet Union. Textbook for higher juridical studies. Edited by N. G. Alexandrov and D. M. Genkin.

37. N. G. Alexandrov, G. K. Moskalenko: *Sovetskoye trudovoye pravo.* 1947.—TheLabour Laws of the Soviet Union. Textbook for law schools.

38. *Sovetskoye trudovoye pravo.* 1949.—The Labour Laws of the Soviet Union. Textbook for juridical institutes and the law faculties of the universities. Edited by N. G. Alexandrov.

References in the text to 'The Labour Laws of the Soviet Union' are to this book.

39. *Voprosy trudovogo prava.* I. Moskva-Leningrad 1948.—Questions of labour law. Published by the Soviet Union's Academy of Sciences. Contains papers by V. M. Dogadov, etc.

40. A. E. Pasherstnik: *Pravovye voprosy voznagrazhdeniya za trud rabochikh i sluzashchikh.* Moskva-Leningrad 1949.—Legal questions concerning the remuneration for the work of workers and employees.

41. *Sovetskoye pravo v period velikoi otechestvennoi voini.* I–II. 1948.—Soviet law during the period of the great national war. Edited by I. T. Golyakov.

42. *Ugolovnoye pravo. Obshchaya chast.* 1948.—Penal law. General part. Textbook for juridical institutes and law faculties. Edited by V. D. Menshagin.

43. V. D. Menshagin, Z. A. Vischinskaya: *Sovetskoye ugolovnoye pravo.* 1950.—The Soviet Union's Penal Code. Textbook for law schools.

44. N. D. Durmanov: *Ponatye prestupleniya.* 1948.—The concept of crime.

45. B. P. Veselovsky: *Kurs ekonomiki i planirovaniya kommunalnogo khozhaistva.* 1945.—Course in the economics and planning of municipal economies.

46. D. L. Broner: *Kurs zhilichnogo khozhaistva.* 1948. Course in housing economics.

47. V. P. Maslakov, N. L. Filatov, V. V. Barmin: *Finansirovanie zhilichno-kommunalnogo khozhaistva.* 1948.—The financing of housing and municipal economies.

48.—A. A. Zaslavsky: *Zhilichno-kommunalnoye khozhaistvo SSSR.* 1948.—Housing and municipal economy in the Soviet Union.

49. M. M. Lifits: *Sovetskaya torgovlya.* 1948. Soviet commerce.

50. L. N. Steinberg: *Planirovanie truda v roznichnoi torgovle.* 1948.—Planning of work in retail trade.

51. F. A. Maximenko: *Ekonomika i planirovanie obshchestvennogo pitaniya.* 1949.—The economics and planning of places of public refreshment. Textbook for trade middle schools.

52. V. V. Kuznetsov: *Otchetny doklad na X syezde profsoyuzov SSSR o rabote V Ts P S.* 1949. Report on the work of unions' Central Council to the All-Union Trade Congress.

53. '*Ustav professionalnykh soyuzov SSSR*'. Rules and regulations for the trade union organizations in the Soviet Union. Published in the periodical *Professionalnye soyuzy* 1949: 5.

54. *Materialy po zakluchenyu kollektivnykh dogorov na 1947 god.* 1947. Material concerning the conclusion of collective agreements for the year 1947. Published by the publishing house of trade unions' Central Council, Profizdat.

55. *Postanovleniya plenumov V Ts S P S.* 1949. Resolutions of the plenum of the trade unions' Central Council.

56. *Kontrol nad raschetami po zarabotnoi plate.* 1948.—Edited by the head of the wages department of the All-Union Central Council, A. P. Stepanov.

57. *Uchet i otchetnost po budzetu gosudarstvennogo sotsialnogo strachovaniya.* 1948.—Book-keeping and auditing as concerns the budget of the State social insurance. Handbook for the trade unions.

58. *Obshchestvenny kontrol profsoyuzov nad rabotoi stolovykh, magazinov i podsobnykh khozaistv.* 1949. The trade unions' social control of work at dining-rooms, shops and in auxiliary agriculture. Published by Profizdat, the publishing house of the All-Union Central Council.

59. Anna Kuznetsova: *Po normam 1950 goda.* 1948.—According to the norms of 1950. Autobiography.

60. *Meditsinskaya pomoshch v Moskve.* 1947.—Medical aid in Moscow. Contains information for the guidance of the public about the different kinds of establishments for medical attention.

61. *Ofitsialny ukazatel passazhirskikh soobshcheny.* 1949. Communications tables.

62. *Bolshaya sovetskaya entsiklopedia.*—Great Soviet Encyclopædia. Special volume: ' Soyuz sovetskikh sotsialisticheskikh respublik '—the Soviet Union. 1948.

63. *Soobshchenie gosudastvennogo planovogo komiteta SSSR i tsentralnogo statisticheskogo upravleniya SSSR ob itogach vypolneniya chetvertogo (pervogo poslevoyennogo) pyatiletnego plana SSR na 1946–1950 gody.* 1951.—Report on the fulfilment of the Five-Year Plan for 1946–1950.

64. A. J. Wyschinski: *Ueber die Sowjetjustiz.* 1939.

65. Y. N. Medinsky: *Public education in the USSR.* 1951.

66. A. Baykov: *The development of the Soviet economic system.* 1946.

67. S. N. Prokopovicz: *Russlands Volkswirtschaft unter den Sowjets.* Zürich, 1944. Contains statistical material with the official sources given.

68. *Narodnoye khozhaistvo SSSR.*—The industry and commerce of the Soviet Union. Four volumes have appeared (1948 to 1951). Contains articles from various periodicals and official material, inter alia reports from the Central Statistical Office.

69. V. M. Dogadov: ' Etapy razvitiya sovetskogo kollektivnogo dogovora'.—Stages in the development of the soviet collective agreement. Article in *Izvestia Akademii Nauk SSSR, Otdelenie ekonomiki i prava,* 1948: 2.

70. V. M. Dogadov: 'K voprosu o subyektakh sovetskogo kollektivnogo dogovora i ego pravovoi sile '.—On the subject matter of the collective agreement and its legality. Article in *Izvestia Akademii Nauk SSSR, Otdelenie ekonomiki i prava,* 1950: 3.

71. E. Manevich: 'Novye stimuly k trudu i zarabotnaya plata pri sotsializme'.—The new incentives to work and the wages of work under socialism. Article in *Voprosy ekonomiki,* 1948: 10.

72. E. Mochova: ' Gosudarstvennye trudovye rezervy—osnovnoi istochnik popolnenia rabochego klassa v SSSR '.—State labour reserves—the most important source for complementing the working-class in the Soviet Union. Article in *Voprosy ekonomiki,* 1949: 4.

73. 'Osnovnye printsipy postroyenia zarabotnoi plati rabochikh'.
—Fundamental principles for the structure of workers' wages.
Article in *V pomoshch FZMK* 1948: 13.

74. 'Pensionnoye obespechenie rabochikh sluzashchikh i chle-
nov ikh seme'.—Pensions for workers and employees and
the members of their families. Article in *V pomoshch profsoyuznomu aktivu* 1951: 19.

75. 'Posobia po vremennoi netrudosposobnosti.'—Assistance on
temporary loss of ability to work. Articles in *V pomoshch profsoyuznomu aktivu* 1950: 22, 23.

76. *Projekt vtorogo pyatiletnego plana razvitiya narodnogo khozhaistva SSSR (1933–1937 gg.) 1934.*—Draft for the second
Five-Year Plan for the development of the national economy
of the Soviet Union 1933–1937. Published by the State planning commission of the Council of People's Commissars.

77. *Slovar-spravochnik po sotsialno-ekonomicheskoi statistike.* 1948.
Reference book of social and economic statistics. Published
by the Central Office of Statistics.

DAILY PAPERS

Izvestia — Pravda — Trud — Vechernyaya Moskva.

PERIODICALS

*Bolshevik — Voprosy ekonomiki — Planovoye khozhaistvo —
Professionalnye soyuzy — V pomoshch FZMK — V pomoshch
profsoyuznomu aktivu — Izvestia Akademii Nauk SSSR.
Otdelenie ekonomiki i prava — Nyheter fran Sovietunionen*
(Stockholm).

INDEX